To Pam O'Too

In memory of Florrie

GOD'S TRIANGLE

Ian D. Richardson

Best wishes,

Ian Richardson

First edition. Published in March 2012
by
RICHARDSON MEDIA LIMITED
26 Ascott Avenue, London W5 5QB, United Kingdom
http://www.richardsonmedia.co.uk/
http://www.godstriangle.com

Cover design: Sally Wright Design, Hobart, Tasmania
http://www.sallywrightdesign.com/

Content editor and layout: Rosemary Richardson

Printed by: Blissetts, Roslin Road, London W3 8DH

ISBN: 978-0-9571401-0-3

ABOUT THE AUTHOR

Ian Richardson was born in the Australian town of Wonthaggi, Victoria, back when it was best known for its State Coal Mine. He grew up in Charlton in North-Central Victoria, where his parents had a printing and newspaper publishing business. He joined the family business on leaving school at the age of 16, not long before his father, John, died at an early age from cancer. Several years later, after his widowed mother re-married and sold the business, he switched to broadcast journalism, first with *Radio 3BO* in Bendigo (where he met his wife Rosemary) then with *Radio Melbourne 3AW*.

Late in 1968, Ian and Rosemary set out for London, for what was initially intended to be a relatively short visit. But Ian was offered a job in the news department of *BBC World Service* at Bush House in London. This led to his spending almost 30 years on the BBC staff. In his latter years with the corporation, he moved into editorial management and project work, spending periods in charge of *BBC World Service* reporters and correspondents, as a senior editor of *BBC World News* television, and as the founding editor of *BBC Arabic Television*.

Both Ian and Rosemary have a keen interest in their respective family histories in the United Kingdom and Australia, and it was this interest that took them to the story of *God's Triangle*.

THANKS

Firstly to my wife, Rosemary, for her considerable support and detective work over the years with *God's Triangle*. This is not a lazy, courtesy appreciation, as she did a great deal of the early research. Further, she edited the content and advised on the layout.

My initial intention was that *God's Triangle* be turned into a feature film, but Rosemary always felt that the story first needed to be written down in detail for the historical record. She was right. This book is the result.

I am also immensely grateful for the help given by Rosalind Gooden, a former Director of Personnel for the *Australian Baptist Missionary Society*. Although we have often approached this story from different perspectives, I have been hugely impressed by her determination to support the historical truth, even if some people might prefer it to stay hidden.

Tribute must also be paid to the women who have the same rare condition as my great aunt. A number of them kindly contacted me in response to a request for advice on what my great aunt's life must have been like. These women wish to remain anonymous because even today they do not feel that society will fully sympathise with, or truly understand, their circumstances.

Thanks must go also to Paul Paice, the only child of Frank Paice and his second wife, Olga. The story that I am about to tell was as much a surprise to him as it was to the rest of us, but he generously helped my research as much as he was able and always treated me with the greatest courtesy and friendship as the sometimes-uncomfortable story unfolded. Sadly, Paul died in August 2011 after a long battle with cancer.

Finally, I must mention the Australian film producer, Roslyn Walker of *Walker Films*, who has unstintingly supported *God's Triangle* right from the time I first approached her in 1998, when she was in charge of script development for *Film Victoria*. Though a cinematic version of *God's Triangle* may still be some time away, Roslyn's mentoring has provided me with the necessary encouragement to stick with the project. Without her, I might well have given up.

CONTENTS

Front cover illustrations:
   Frank and Florence Paice, A. Olga Johnston
Back cover illustrations:
   Ian Richardson, Faridpur Baptist Mission House (top), Rural scene,
   Bengal (middle), Baptist Gospel Hall, Mymensingh (bottom).
Book illustrations:

INTRODUCTION

This is the story of Florence Martha Cox.

"Florrie", as she was widely known, was my great aunt. She died in Melbourne, Australia, in 1950, understanding little of the circumstances that destroyed her marriage and her life as a Baptist missionary in East Bengal (now Bangladesh). It is also an account of an establishment cover-up of the events surrounding her failed marriage, and of how her husband, the Rev. Frank E. Paice, and his second wife, Olga Johnston, erased a whole chunk of their past.

The story reveals much about the social constraints of an age when strict Christian virtues and rigid social taboos reigned supreme over intelligent and open discussion and a realisation that life's problems must not be viewed simply as black or white, or Christian good versus evil.

God's Triangle is about my search for the truth surrounding my great aunt. The story would have remained a secret, had it not been for my mother casually showing me a photograph that excited my incurable journalistic curiosity.

I was brought up in a staunchly-Protestant environment, but I am no longer a believer, nor have I been since my late teenage years. Hence, this story is viewed through the prism of an atheist, but I hope believers will accept that I have done my best to tell the story with honesty and fairness.

My great aunt and her fellow Christian missionaries in India were mostly kind souls who genuinely believed that they had a God-given mission to link "doing good" with spreading the word of the Lord and obtaining conversions, heedless of the cost to themselves or the converts.

To Florrie's credit, there is evidence that her emphasis was more on "doing good" than on "saving souls", although she was a passionate believer and would have applauded a world that was entirely Christian. Many modern missionaries now accept that proselytising in non-Christian countries is offensive and, sometimes, against local law. They, therefore, prefer to be Christians by example rather than campaigning evangelists.

As part of the cover-up some years later, most of the related official documents were lost or destroyed by the Baptist Church. All that remains in the church records are a few cryptic minutes from board meetings of the Baptist Foreign Mission Board in 1918 and 1919.

The families involved in events that I will recount also destroyed their records, or at least hid them where they hoped they wouldn't be

1

found. As I will explain later, it was only by an extraordinary accident that I came across what appeared to be the sole surviving photograph of Florrie Cox's wedding.

Had it not been for old copies of the missionary magazines, *The Southern Baptist*, *Our Indian Field* and *Our Bond*, held in Baptist archives in Melbourne and in Oxford, England, it would have been impossible to get to the truth. The magazines themselves did not refer to any scandal, of course, but they did provide vital dates and other clues that helped my wife and me assemble a jigsaw.

A jigsaw is a perfect analogy for how our research progressed. Not all the pieces could be found. However, we were able over the years to put together a reasonably complete picture. Sometimes, we would go weeks or months without finding a piece of the jigsaw and even when one was located, it wasn't always possible to know where it fitted.

It would have been nice to assemble the *God's Triangle* jigsaw in an orderly manner, say, bottom up or top down, but it was never going to be like that. Sometimes we would find a big chunk of the picture but not fully understand what it portrayed. And sometimes we would fail to spot the obvious, or would be led off on a false trail.

A vital part of the jigsaw was provided by the divorce file for Great Aunt Florrie and Frank Paice. But as you will learn, the divorce papers were part of the cover-up and far from easy to obtain.

The depth of the embarrassment and anxiety that erupted around Florrie Cox, Frank Paice and Olga Johnston cannot be overstated. Worst of all, it tore apart the Paice family and spilled over into my own branch of the Cox family, even though Great Aunt Florrie was arguably an entirely innocent party.

My mother was initially very unsure about the propriety of my research, but became a supporter of the project after reading an early draft of the story. An aunt once demanded to know "what purpose will be served?" by my ferreting around the events, but she, too, later gave me her support and provided some very useful background material. The greatest opposition came from an uncle, now deceased, who had an almost congenital hostility to anything to do with family histories. "Leave sleeping dogs lie," he firmly told me more than once. But he later agreed to read a draft of the story and withdrew his opposition.

I have some sympathy for the reasons why the events I am about to recount were felt to be too sensitive for public consumption, and I will come to that later. But it is depressing that 80 years after the event, Florrie's divorce records — uniquely as far as I can tell — were still marked "closed for all time".

The path of this story may sometimes meander, but there is a reason for this and I hope you will find it an engrossing tale.

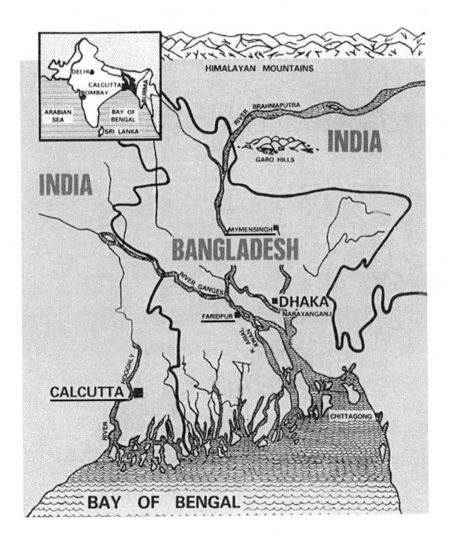

THE FAMILY CONNECTIONS

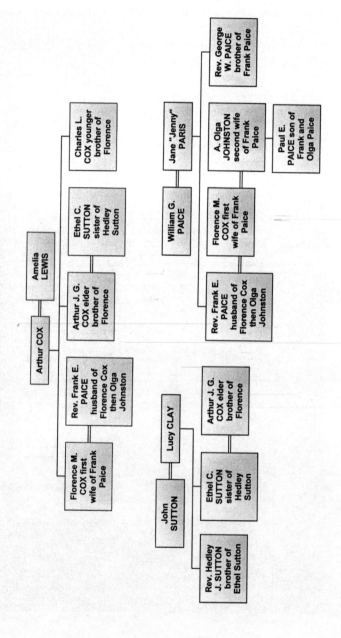

Arthur COX

Amelia LEWIS

Arthur J. G. COX elder brother of Florence

Ethel C. SUTTON sister of Hedley Sutton

Charles L. COX younger brother of Florence

Rev. Frank E. PAICE husband of Florence Cox then Olga Johnston

Florence M. COX first wife of Frank Paice

John SUTTON

Lucy CLAY

Ethel C. SUTTON sister of Hedley Sutton

Arthur J. G. COX elder brother of Florence

Rev. Hedley J. SUTTON brother of Ethel Sutton

Rev. Frank E. PAICE husband of Florence Cox then Olga Johnston

Florence M. COX first wife of Frank Paice

William G. PAICE

Jane "Jenny" PARIS

A. Olga JOHNSTON second wife of Frank Paice

Rev. George W. PAICE brother of Frank Paice

Paul E. PAICE son of Frank and Olga Paice

WHO WAS WHO IN GOD'S TRIANGLE

Before proceeding with this story, it makes sense to provide some background to the three main characters: Florence Cox, the Rev. Frank Paice and Olga Johnston, and also to the senior Baptist missionary in East Bengal, the Rev. Hedley Sutton. There were others involved, of course, but I will come to them as required and as the story progresses.

Florence Martha "Florrie" Cox (later Paice)
1887-1950

Florrie Cox was born at home in the Melbourne suburb of Richmond on November 5, 1887, the third of six children born to Arthur and Amelia Cox.

It was a very religious family – extremely so in the case of some members. Amelia was very strict, with church-going, hymns, prayers and reading the bible being the only activities permitted on Sundays. Even the meals were prepared the day before. There were complaints in the family about the time Amelia devoted to church activities, often to the detriment to her perceived responsibilities as a mother and housewife. It was as though she were acquiring credit points to ensure her place in Heaven.

I have not been able to learn anything significant about Florrie's father, Arthur, as he had died before any of his surviving descendants were old enough to absorb impressions of him.

Florrie had two brothers, Arthur and Charles. Her sisters were, in order of birth, Amelia (known as "Minnie", perhaps to differentiate her from her mother), Alice and Lois.

The two brothers could hardly have been less alike. Arthur was my grandfather and was a forceful, intolerant, humourless, status-conscious, hypocritical and sometimes-violent man with few friends. His religious fervour led him into several bouts of insanity that required hospital treatment. During the Second World War, he was diagnosed with religious mania and dismissed as a major in the Australian Army after declaring to his men that he was Jesus Christ's second-in-command.

By contrast, his younger brother Charles – universally known as "Charlie" – was a polite and placid businessman who never forced his views on anyone. He had no interest in religion and attended church

5

very rarely and only when pushed to do so by his wife. By all accounts, he was widely liked and admired.

Florrie Cox's sisters, Minnie and Alice, were both married with children, while her sister Lois battled tuberculosis throughout her teenage years before dying when just 22.

Little else is known of the three sisters, nor has it been possible to establish exactly what Florrie Cox was like in her early years. She was, though, sufficiently religious to become a Sunday School teacher and later to take on the considerable burdens of a missionary wife in one of the more arduous and remote postings the Baptist Church could offer.

Florrie was unusually tall for a woman in that era — about six feet or 183cms. She became engaged to Frank Paice when she was 24, which would have been considered rather late. In those days, women who weren't "fixed up" to be married by their early twenties were usually fearful of being left "on the shelf", and as spinsters, were often viewed as unfulfilled persons.

On the other hand, men who did not marry would be referred to, often with affection and respect, as "confirmed bachelors". The strong possibility that many of these men were closet homosexuals did not seem to be considered.

In the light of what we know about Florrie's mother and other conservative members of that family, there must have been great joy that she was to be married – and not just married to anyone, but married to a Man of God and a missionary.

There is no precise record of when Frank and Florrie were engaged, but the indications are that it was not long before Frank sailed for India in October, 1912.

Though society contained pockets of uninhibited licentiousness in the early 1900s, sexual attitudes for most people – particularly staunch Christians – were very rigid and oppressive. Married women could expect to have many pregnancies in their reproductive life, but they would be told little about the "facts of life", as sexual knowledge was euphemistically called.

The more liberal-minded families might offer a newly-married woman a book on "married women's health". These books touched on reproductive matters, but were usually very coy and often ill-informed. (One such book included the "fact" that the best way to avoid pregnancies was to engage in conjugal relations midway between the monthly periods.) It was widely felt that wives should simply follow the lead of their husbands in the marital bed, though in the majority of cases, their husbands were almost as anxious and sexually ignorant as their wives.

The only truly effective form of contraception was abstinence. This was not seen by devout Christian women as a burden, as it was considered very unladylike to enjoy sex, or at least to admit to enjoying it. I remember overhearing elderly female relatives declaring that it was important for married women to "maintain Christian standards in the bedroom".

I took this to mean that any sexual activity should be confined to the so-called "missionary position" with the man always on top in the traditional manner. These standards would also require that any nudity be as discreet as possible. (One of my Cox family aunts once proudly declared that her husband had never seen her naked.)

The accepted attitude of married women towards sex — not helped by the fear of yet another pregnancy — often had a discouraging impact on their husbands. Even in my youth in the 1950s, it was quite common for married men to dismiss sex as "an over-rated indoor sport".

To avoid being carried away by sexual desires, courting couples in the early 1900s were normally not allowed to be alone together until such time as they became engaged. When they went out together on a date, they would be required to do so with a chaperone.

Keeping this in mind, Florrie and Frank would have had no opportunities for sexual encounters or exploration of each other's bodies before Frank left Australia. Even when Florrie joined him in Calcutta two years later, she and her fiancé would have been allowed little or no time together. Nor, as devout Christians, would they have wanted it any other way.

If the social and sexual climate had been more relaxed – dare I say, enlightened – it is quite possible that the marriage between Frank and Florrie would never have taken place. However, given their status in the community and the laws of that time, breaking off an engagement was almost as difficult as a divorce is today. One or other of the parties could have sued for "breach of promise". This was something not treated lightly by the courts and often ended up with public humiliation in the newspapers and the payment of financial compensation by the offending party.

Rev. Frank Ernest Paice
1888-1964

Frank Paice was also born into a religious family — in Woolston, a suburb of Christchurch, New Zealand. His parents, William George "Willie" and Jane "Jenny" Paice, both born in England, had their first child in Australia, at South Melbourne in 1878. They then spent at least the next eight years in New Zealand, where they had a second daughter, Eva, followed by George and finally Frank.

It has not been possible to establish when, or why, the family returned to Australia, but Frank was brought up near Melbourne at One Tree Hill in the Dandenongs, where Willie had a market garden and was a lay preacher in the Baptist Church.

Frank grew into a handsome young man with a natural, commanding presence. Though he was a man of firm and clear views, he was mostly well liked, finding it easy to mix with a variety of friends and associates. He was a skilled carpenter but initially trained to become an engineer. He never completed his engineering studies after both he and his elder brother George "got God's call" and chose to become clergymen, doing their training together at the Baptist College of Victoria in Melbourne.

A formal photograph published in *The Southern Baptist* in June 1911 (see page 17) shows the students and lecturers lined up at the college with Frank and George standing alongside each other. One of the lecturers in that photograph was my great uncle, the Rev. Hedley J. Sutton, who was in Melbourne on an extended furlough (leave) from his missionary responsibilities in East Bengal.

It can be assumed that it was Hedley who inspired Frank to join him on the mission field. Frank also felt attracted to India because his grandfather, George T. Paice, had fought in the Second Sikh War of 1848-49 which had resulted in the Punjab being annexed by Britain.

While Frank's brother, George W. Paice, took up the first of several postings to churches in Victoria, Frank underwent extra training to prepare him for his work in East Bengal. It was apparently during this time that he began courting Florrie Cox. They almost certainly met through being members of the congregation at the Auburn Baptist

Church, which was a religious and informal social hub in Melbourne for the Cox, Sutton and Paice families.

It is difficult to know what drew Frank and Florrie together. Frank wanted to marry and have children, but to what extent this desire was matched by Florrie cannot be established. Whatever Florrie's attitude, she would have been under family and social pressures to marry and produce children.

Frank would not have had a wide choice of potential wives as few women would have been sufficiently religious and hardy enough to accept the many challenges of a missionary wife.

It is not known if Frank had any serious girlfriends before he became engaged to Florrie, but I stumbled across an intriguing entry in an illustrated autograph book that my mother inherited from her aunt Maude Irene "Rena" Sutton, one of Hedley Sutton's younger sisters.

Rena died in March 1911, from tuberculosis, aged just 22. Frank's entry, like most of the others, had a religious and formal tone. But it did show that he knew Rena back in February 1910, the year before he began studying for the ministry and more than two years before he became engaged to Florrie.

It is not now possible to establish whether there was any special significance to this entry, but my mother thought that there could well have been. She said that single men did not routinely make entries in an unmarried girl's autograph book unless they were family or close friends. It is entirely possible, therefore, that Frank had seen Rena as a potential marriage partner.

We will never know for certain about Frank's intentions towards Rena, but it is clear that she would have been sufficiently religious to qualify as a missionary wife. I have in my possession an *Active Member's Pledge Card* signed by Rena as a member of the evangelical group, Junior Society of Christian Endeavour, when she was a teenager. In addition to the usual daily prayers, she promised to read the bible each day and carry out other regular religious duties.

It is very likely that Hedley Sutton, an elder brother, would have been delighted to have a member of his own family alongside him in East Bengal "serving God by gathering souls", as it was often put. But it was not to be.

The speculation about Frank and Rena aside, it is ironical, in view of what happened later to Frank, that his contribution to Rena's autograph book should include this quotation from the former British Prime Minister, Benjamin Disraeli: "Circumstances are beyond the control of men, but his conduct is within his own power".

Alvina Olga "Olga" Johnston (later Paice)
1884-1966

Olga Johnston was the child of immigrant parents. Her father, Abraham Johnston, was an agricultural labourer in Southern Ireland. Her mother, Maria Dorothea Juliane "Julia" Holzgrefe, was born near Hanover in Germany.

It was a double wedding for Julia and her elder sister, Wilhelmina. It took place in November 1869 at the home of the girls' father, Christoph, near Carapook, a farming area between Coleraine and Casterton in Victoria. The service was conducted by an Evangelical Lutheran clergyman, but the Johnston family were Church of England.

Julia was just 17 when she was married. Her sister was 20. The wedding register gave Abraham's age as 31, but other records make it clear that he was 38 or 39.

Despite the sexual restrictions I have already mentioned, it seems likely that Julia was pregnant at the time of her marriage, as the first-born arrived less than seven months after the wedding. In all, Julia bore Abraham eight children, the last of whom was Olga, born on September 20, 1884, at Carapook.

Not much is known about Julia (sometimes also called Julia Anna), other than that she died aged just 37 in July 1889 when Olga was only four years old, leaving her and some of the other younger siblings to be brought up by their father and eldest sister, Dora.

Quite a bit of information is available about Abraham, thanks chiefly to an obituary in the *Portland Guardian* of May 16, 1921. From this, we discover that he was a tough and resourceful character.

The obituary recounts that when Abraham was setting out for Australia from Liverpool on the *City of Lincoln* in 1852, the ship's owners went bankrupt. Abraham and his fellow passengers seized control of the ship with the intention of sailing it to Melbourne, where they intended selling it to recover their expenses.

This escapade, with its unpredictable consequences, became unnecessary when the vessel was bought by another firm of ship owners and the voyage took place without further incident.

Before settling down to farming at Carapook, Abraham unsuccessfully sought riches as a prospector on the goldfields of Bendigo, Ballarat and Dunolly, among other places.

For a time he went into business using a horse and dray to transport flour around the Bendigo and Ballarat areas.

There are no records of how the Johnston family coped with the death of Julia. Nor is it clear whether religion played a major part in their lives. At some point, Olga switched from the Church of England to become a devout Baptist. Those who might have been able to tell me about Olga's time as a girl and as a young woman have long since died.

What *is* known is that Olga trained as a nurse at Melbourne's Women's Hospital — later renamed the Royal Women's Hospital — before moving to Geelong to be with her sister Dora and other members of her family.

While in Geelong, Olga began attending the Aberdeen Street Baptist Church, which had a reputation for evangelical fervour. It is there that she would have met and come under the persuasive influence of Hedley Sutton, who preached there from time to time while on furlough in Australia. Church records show that Olga was accepted for missionary training in September 1911.

It is not known whether Olga had any marriage prospects before becoming a missionary, but by the time she arrived in East Bengal in 1912, she was already 28 — very late for most women of that era to get married. As there would be few suitable Christian men available for marriage in East Bengal, she had no doubt resigned herself to spinsterhood.

Olga's nursing skills would have been much valued on the missionary field, not just by the mission staff, but also as a means of drawing in the local population to expose them to the Christian message as they were given medical assistance and advice. Being a former farm girl would also have helped her cope with the physical adversities she would face in East Bengal.

A photograph taken of Olga as she was about to set out for East Bengal showed her to be pretty and having a pleasant demeanour. But as the years went by, she gained a reputation as a forceful, rather intimidating and bitter character. She had strong views on many subjects and was not inhibited from expressing them.

Rev. Hedley John Sutton
1876-1946

Much is known about my missionary great uncle, Hedley Sutton, for reasons that I will explain shortly. He was a man of exceptional intellect and from a large and fairly ordinary family. In some respects he could be seen as a marginal player in the story of *God's Triangle*, but in truth his involvement was significant.

There were two chief reasons for this: 1) he was the most senior Baptist missionary in East Bengal at the time Frank, Florrie and Olga were there, and 2) Hedley and Florrie were members of the same extended family. (Hedley's sister, Ethel, was married to Florrie's brother, Arthur junior.)

Hedley's parents, John and Lucy Sutton, emigrated to Melbourne from Lincolnshire, England, where John was an agricultural labourer. He worked for many years for the Hawthorn City Council, doing labouring jobs, including sweeping the streets. He was hard working and financially astute and at one point owned three houses.

John was, by all accounts, a severe, very religious and daunting man, with little understanding of the many children he had fathered. By contrast, Lucy was considered warm and affectionate. Nonetheless, Hedley felt aggrieved that his mother was much less keen than his father on his pursuing academic studies.

Hedley was the seventh of 12 children born to John and Lucy. His education began at the Auburn State School before he became a student of Wesley College then Melbourne University's Trinity College by virtue of hard-won scholarships.

Hedley grew up to be austere, hard-working, hugely-competitive and rather self-centred. His competitive spirit was obvious not just from his academic studies but as a keen amateur footballer.

As a college and university student, Hedley was forever conscious that he was a labourer's son mixing with the privileged children of the prominent and wealthy. This rankled, especially as the scholarship money had to be supplemented by part-time jobs, tutoring fees, loans from his father and prizes from educational competitions.

Hedley's primary interests, aside from his faith, were the classics and languages. Immediately after graduation from Melbourne University with an honours degree in his early twenties, he was appointed classics master at Brighton Grammar in Melbourne, a post he held for five years.

Hedley had been brought up as a Methodist, but in his matriculation year at Wesley College, he transferred his religious commitment to the Baptists and remained with them for the rest of his life.

This conversion to the Baptist faith led to his training as a missionary at Ormond College in Melbourne. He was ordained in November 1903 and sailed later that month for a missionary life in East Bengal. Apart from two periods of furlough, he remained there until 1927.

Hedley's second furlough was primarily to marry Miss Elsie Luke, a daughter of a respected and financially-comfortable Australian family. She was a niece of Aeneas Gunn who wrote the Australian classic *We of the Never Never* and a cousin of Sir Hudson Fysh, a co-founder of the Australian airline, *Qantas*.

Hedley and Elsie became friends through her role as secretary of the Baptist Women's Missionary Union. By the time they married in Melbourne in June 1920, Hedley was about to turn 44 and Elsie was 49. Elsie accompanied Hedley back to Mymensingh in East Bengal in November the following year, but could not adapt to the hardships and health hazards routinely faced by a missionary wife. She returned to Australia in poor health early in 1927, to be followed late that year by Hedley, who then resigned as a missionary.

Hedley had been heavily involved during his 1920/21 furlough in plans to set up a Baptist school in Melbourne to honour the memory of the missionary William Carey. Carey Grammar was established in 1923 and on Hedley's resignation from the missionary service, he was appointed Vice-Principal. He held that post until retiring in 1941.

Hedley was rather unworldly and did not seem to be a man in danger of being overwhelmed by lustful thoughts about the opposite sex. In his youth, he did have a friendship with an Emily Winstone who lived in the Melbourne area. This did not appear to be an intimate affair and Emily went on to marry someone else.

When Hedley was in his early forties, still single and working in Mymensingh, he produced *Hedley–His Story*, a lengthy part-work about his life before becoming a missionary.

It was hand-written for Elsie's private consumption, but found its way into the archives at Carey Grammar. Hedley would sign off each chapter in this private autobiography with "Elsie's loving lover,

Hedley" or "Hedley Dah". There was no indication, otherwise, that he was writing to the woman who was to become his wife, though to be fair, I did find one rather obtuse love poem that he once sent to Elsie.

Hedley's siblings were barely mentioned in his life story — the first reference, half way through, was a passing one to a sister, Lydia — and at no time did he mention that another sister, Ethel, was married to Florrie Cox's brother, Arthur. But there were a number of affectionate references to his friendship with Emily Winstone. There was no indication that he thought Elsie might regard this as a little insensitive.

The structure and content of his autobiography was curious and revealed unintended sides to Hedley's character. He wrote almost entirely in the third person. In other words, "Hedley did this", "Hedley did that", rather than use the word "I" or "me".

It could be argued that this was from a sense of modesty, but there is little modesty on display in his life story. Indeed, he seemed rather pleased with himself. At the same time, there was an underlying sense of grievance about the attitude of his parents towards him and his achievements and the snobbery he encountered as a student.

There was the revealing entry he made in my mother's autograph book in 1929: "To learn what to love and what to hate, what to honour and what to despise, is the purpose of education". A truly astonishing thing to claim, not least for a teacher and devout Christian. Thus the cumulative effect of Hedley's austere, rather self-centred character suggests to me that he was not emotionally well equipped to deal with the events of *God's Triangle*.

Hedley, who died in Melbourne in February 1946, had an impressive impact on Carey Grammar, particularly in its early days, and a whole section of the school's archive has been devoted to his life and his works. His contribution to society is further commemorated by having a Baptist retirement community in Camberwell, Melbourne, named after him. Unfortunately, his writings – at least the ones that have survived – contained no references to Florrie or the cover-up.

Florence Martha "Florrie" Cox — Melbourne 1914

The Cox family — Melbourne 1914
Back row: Charles, Florence, Arthur, "Minnie". Seated: Alice,
Amelia and Arthur Snr. Framed photograph on floor:
Lois (deceased)

THE SOUTHERN BAPTIST

June 29th, 1911.

By courtesy "Punch".

LECTURERS AND STUDENTS, BAPTIST COLLEGE OF VICTORIA. SESSION 1911.

Top Row.—R. Thorne, P. Goodman, E. Holloway, W. Wingfield, A. Hannah, J. Newnham, A. Muriel, A. Parker, S. Goble.

Second Top Row.—A. Driver, T. Kelly, C. Urquhart, F. Paice, G. Paice, S. Bunn, R. Stowards, S. M'Donald.

Second Front Row.—S. Dorman, J. Howlett-Ross, Rev. F. C. Spurr, Rev. W. H. Holdsworth, M.A. (president), Miss Sims, B.A.

Rev. Hedley Sutton, M.A., Rev. E. Harris.

Front Row.—C. Harris, H. Childs, W. Phillips, J. M'Cue, E. Fisher.

VOL. XVIII. No. 38   MELBOURNE AND ADELAIDE, SEPTEMBER 12, 1912.   5/- PER ANNUM; 5/6 POSTED.

Victorian Baptist Foreign Mission

Our Outgoing Missionaries

DATES OF SAILING

October 2nd—Revs. Hedley Sutton, M.A., and F. E. Paice
October 8th—Miss C. Williams and Miss Olga Johnston

- - GREAT - -

Farewell Meeting

Monday, Sept. 16th, 1912

Collins Street Church

Chairman - - REV. J. H. GOBLE

Commence at 7.45 p.m. sharp

Collection for Forward Policy

Miss Olga Johnston

Miss C. Williams

Ordination & Designation Service to
Rev. F. E. Paice
— and —
Miss Olga Johnston,
7.45

Address
Rev. F. E. Harry

Response by the two
Missionaries

Prayer
Rev. W. H. Holdsworth, M.A.

Rev. F. E. Paice

Valedictory Services
to
Missionaries
returning after
furlough

Farewell Address
Rev. J. H. Goble

Response
Miss C. Williams
Rev. Hedley Sutton,
M.A.

Rev. Hedley Sutton, M. A.

Forward Policy Aim, £3100.   Present Attainment, £2088

Wanted by October 5th, £1112

18

Frank and Florence Paice after their wedding at the
Circular Road, Baptist Chapel, Calcutta, December 1914

Frank and Olga Paice after their marriage in Calcutta in 1919
and at a mayoral ball in Melbourne in 1952

1 In the beginning

God's Triangle had its genesis in March, 1997. I was in Australia and staying with my mother, Rena Wood, who had been widowed for a second time and was living in the Melbourne suburb of Blackburn. Mum was keen on the family history, but was never organised sufficiently to assemble it in any logical order.

One afternoon, as we sifted our way through boxes of old family photos — most of them unidentified — my attention was caught by a formal group photo taken in a studio (see Page 16). It was of her grandparents, Arthur and Amelia Cox, with their children and we worked out that it was taken either in 1913 or 1914.

I recognised my grandfather, Arthur J. G. Cox, and his younger brother, Charlie, but not their three sisters in the group. One of these was a taller-than-average, slim, dark-haired woman. My mother dismissively identified her as "Oh, that's just Aunty Florrie".

It should be noted at this point that my mother could sometimes be extremely evasive, never willingly answering a direct question with a direct answer. But under persistent questioning she would allow things to slip out.

Here is our conversation as best I can remember it:

Me: Aunty Florrie? I didn't know anything about an Aunty Florrie.
Mum: Oh, Aunty Florrie wasn't talked about much.
Me: Oh? Why not?
Mum: Oh, I don't know, Ian. I was just a little girl back then. They just didn't talk about her.
Me: But why not?
Mum: I told you. I don't know. (pause) But she died in Mont Park [a mental asylum in Melbourne].
Me: Well, was she insane, or something?
Mum: Oh, I don't know.

Me: But you must have heard something.

Mum: No, I wasn't told anything. The family didn't talk about her. (pause) But there was something about her marrying a missionary in Bengal and it all going wrong.

Me: What do you mean, 'wrong'?

Mum: Just wrong. (pause) I don't know. (long pause) And there was that other woman.

Me: What other woman?

Mum: Oh, I don't know. The one he had the affair with; the other missionary he married.

By now, my ears were flapping with interest, but my mother had clearly decided I had been told more than enough. She did, though, add just one more snippet before directing the conversation elsewhere: "It was a terrible scandal. Mother told me that it was in the papers, the Melbourne *Truth* [a weekly newspaper much in the mould of Britain's now-defunct *News of the World*]".

We moved on to the rest of the photographs without returning to the intriguing subject of Aunty Florrie.

Despite my interest in the story of my great aunt, I was unable to investigate further before returning to London, but late that year, I was back in Melbourne, by which time I had begun to assemble a very vague outline of Florrie's story.

Then came the first of a series of lucky breaks that marked my research as the years went by.

The first of these emerged when I phoned the headquarters in Melbourne of the Australian Baptist Missionary Union. I was put through to the Director of Personnel, Rosalind Gooden. I told her that I was enquiring about Miss Florence Cox, who had apparently been a Baptist missionary in Bengal during the First World War. There was a pause before she said enigmatically "I think you'd better come in to see me".

Soon after I was welcomed into Rosalind's office in the basement of the Auburn Baptist Church in Burwood Road. She explained that earlier in the year she was awarded her master's degree in theology with a thesis entitled *Awakening Women*, about the influence of Australian women missionaries working overseas for the Baptists.

The period under scrutiny in the thesis ended in 1913, the year before Florrie sailed to India, but Rosalind had become aware of unusual circumstances surrounding my great aunt who had married the Rev. Frank Paice. She was curious to know more. We agreed to keep in touch.

The next thing I learned — though I am no longer sure how — was that Frank Paice had become prominent in local government in suburban Melbourne. Nunawading Council was said to be a good starting point to seek more information about him, so I rang the library and was put through to the local history department.

The woman who answered my call cheerfully informed me that "of course" she had heard of Councillor Frank Paice. To my astonishment, she promptly ran through a summary of his local council achievements that dated back to 1936. They included terms as Shire President of Nunawading, an outer suburb of Melbourne, and after Nunawading became a city, he was elected its Mayor. When I expressed an interest in learning more about Cllr. Paice, she rattled off a telephone number. "Ring that," she instructed. When I enquired whose number it was, I was in for a further surprise: "It's his son, Paul," she informed me, "he's a very nice man who does a lot of voluntary work in the local community".

This stroke of luck left me with a moral dilemma: Should I contact Paul Paice? What if he knew nothing of his father's first marriage? And how would he react to being called out of the blue by a stranger about such a delicate topic?

The following Saturday afternoon I summoned the courage to phone Paul. Fortuitously, he had "just walked in" after interrupting a beach holiday for 24 hours to attend to some business at his local Presbyterian Church. I hesitantly explained that I was researching the life of my great aunt. Was he aware that his father had been married to a Florence Cox in India?

There was a shocked pause as Paul took this in. He then confirmed that his father had been married a long time ago to a Miss Cox, but his father had told him that they had been divorced because "she didn't tell me she couldn't have babies". I asked Paul if he would agree to meet me to talk in more detail about my great aunt Florrie and his father. Paul considered this for a while then told me he wanted to give my call some more thought first. He promised to phone me back before 1.30pm the next day after church and before he and his wife returned to their seaside holiday home.

Clearly, my call had caused Paul some emotional turmoil that left him unsure how to react. The hours went by and at 1.25pm on the Sunday, just as I had resigned myself to not hearing from him, the phone rang. It was Paul telling me he would meet me that afternoon.

At 3pm I walked up to his front door in Blackburn to be met by Paul, a tall and thin man in his seventies, and his wife, Lin. Both the Paices were very courteous, but as was to be expected, cautious. As we sipped tea, Paul said he greatly admired his father, but admitted that he knew very little about the first marriage.

Paul had expressed great surprise in our telephone conversation the previous day that his father Frank, his mother Olga and my great aunt Florrie Cox had all been missionaries together in India. As far as he was aware, his father had always been an engineer and had been employed by Hume's Limited.

This huge Australian engineering company invented the spun concrete pipes that earned it fame and riches around the world. Paul knew that his parents had been in India for a time, but that was when his father was in Calcutta as General Manager of Hume's India division.

Paul, who was born after his parents returned to Australia in 1924, had been brought up as a Presbyterian and had assumed that this was the church his father had always attended. He had not been aware that his father had ever been a Baptist or a missionary. As for his mother, he could not recall her ever going to church and he understood that she did not have any religion.

His mother had been very secretive, Paul told me, and when his father had died, had tried to stop any reference to the first marriage being recorded on the death certificate. "Why do you need to put that in?" she complained. But it went in anyway, as was required by law.

Not surprisingly, the topic of Frank's marriage to Florrie had not got a detailed airing in the Paice family – at least not in the presence of Paul. But Paul did recall once overhearing his father talking on the telephone to a Mr Cox.

The impression he gained from this conversation was that his father had been providing some financial support for my great aunt, but Mr Cox – presumably one of Florrie's brothers, Arthur or Charlie – had said that it was no longer necessary to make any further payments. I later calculated that this call took place around the time when Florrie first entered Mont Park Asylum in 1945 as a voluntary patient.

Gradually my meetings with the Paices became more relaxed as Paul's interest was aroused by the possibility of learning about a previously-unknown part of his parents' lives. He offered to help where he could, but he would have to leave the research to me.

Paul and I parted on good terms with my promising to keep him informed of anything my research uncovered.

Inspections of the newspaper files at the Victorian State Library provided me with more details of Frank Paice's high standing in the community. I also discovered that he was a Freemason — a fact that I felt might be of significance as the *God's Triangle* story unfolded.

Frank was, to resort to a cliché, a pillar of society. Yet, there was not a word in the public record about Frank having been an ordained clergyman or, for six years, a missionary in India.

A return visit to the archives in the basement of the Auburn Baptist Church was also productive. I learn that Frank and Florrie's marriage was celebrated at the Lower Circular Road Baptist Church in Calcutta on Tuesday, December 22, 1914. This was just a month after Florrie had arrived by sea from Australia and as the First World War was developing into *The Great War* with previously-unimaginable casualties on both sides of the conflict.

2 Sex and religion

Sex is a central sub-text of religion, which is mostly about control. The churches exercise this control by exploiting the assumption by many millions of people that they can't have somehow turned up on this earth without a purpose; some mysterious being must have created them and their world with a clear objective in mind.

Originally that control had understandable, sometimes even laudable, reasons. If it were dangerous or unhealthy or merely inadvisable for a totally uneducated people to engage in certain practices, what better way to stop that practice than to invoke the word of an unseen, all-seeing, all-powerful and vengeful god?

It could be argued that if mankind had evolved in such a way that the human reproductive organs could not be easily harmed by infection and could be switched on and off as required, then religion might not have taken such a prescriptive and proscriptive attitude.

The overwhelming majority of religions took the view that the best way to control sexual desires and activities was to imply with varying degrees of insistence that sexual activity was linked to the works of the Devil except within very strict boundaries. Even with the easy availability of condoms and other forms of contraception, this attitude prevails to this day over much of the world's population.

There could hardly be a greater example of the religious attitude to sex than the fiction that Jesus Christ was the result of a virgin birth. By asserting that, it is implied that Jesus and his mother Mary were somehow above the messy and distasteful business of sexual intercourse. It was, therefore, further proof that they were flawless superior beings.

In my childhood in Australia, pregnant women used euphemisms, such as "in the family way" to describe their condition. To reveal that they were pregnant was to tacitly admit that they had "done it" – i.e.

engaged in sexual intercourse – so women went to some lengths to hide a pregnancy for as long as possible.

The Baptist Church, as many other churches still do to this day, took few chances that its missionaries might be led astray by "improper" sexual desires and behaviour. The clothing that missionary women wore said a lot. They wore high-necked dresses with long sleeves and ankle-length skirts. Brassieres were not widely worn back then. Instead, women mostly wore bodices that avoided drawing attention to their breasts. The clothes would have been very hot and uncomfortable in the Indian climate, though having so little skin exposed to view did help reduce the chances of being bitten by malaria-bearing mosquitoes.

There was no question of Florrie Cox being allowed by the church to accompany her fiancé to East Bengal. She would have to patiently wait in Melbourne until the marriage was about to take place.

Such was the nervousness about the risk of unmarried sex that when Hedley Sutton went back to East Bengal in 1912 with his two new recruits and a returning missionary, Miss Constance Williams, they travelled on separate ships. The men, Hedley Sutton and Frank Paice, sailed for Calcutta on one ship, while Olga Johnston and Constance Williams travelled on another steamer six days later. Perhaps there weren't four berths available on the one ship, but that is unlikely. The strict separation of the sexes would have been the primary reason.

Back then, an engagement to marry was intended to allow a couple to get know each other a little more in a non-sexual sense before actual sexual intimacy took place after the wedding. If, by some chance, the couple did fall prey to their sexual desires and the woman became pregnant, the marriage could be discreetly brought forward and the resultant baby passed off as "premature".

Both Frank and Florrie would have wished to "save themselves" sexually for married life, but in any case there were no opportunities for intimacies of any sort because they spent the engagement apart. Perhaps their letters to each other revealed intimate thoughts and actions, but I very much doubt it. That would have been considered too risky, as letters could easily fall into the hands of third parties. Had Frank and Florrie been able to spend their engagement together, there might have been an opportunity for at least some heavy petting. Frank might then have made an important discovery.

3 The commitment to Bengal

Becoming a missionary in foreign parts was a long-term, perhaps lifetime, commitment. It was certainly not to be taken on lightly. Nor was it for the faint-hearted. Yet, reading through the missionary magazines there is little to indicate just how truly difficult life on the field could be.

As far as can be established, Florrie Cox was given no specialist training, as she was going to Bengal as a "missionary wife", rather than as a missionary.

In line with society in general, women on the missionary field usually took a secondary role. The single women who "had the call" were not ordained or trained to anywhere near the same level as the men. And the married women were not officially regarded as missionaries. Theirs was primarily a support role, running the household and supervising the servants while their husbands were out "saving souls".

One thing that was common to all those sent to Bengal by the Baptists was the requirement that they become fluent in the Bengali language, both written and spoken, so they could communicate well with the local populace to help them spread God's word. Hedley Sutton, with a natural aptitude for languages, was noted for his exceptional grasp of the Bengali language and for his translation skills. This leads me on to how Frank Paice might have developed his friendship with Olga Johnston.

It was the usual practice for new missionaries to spend their first two years of service concentrating on their Bengali language skills and there are references in *Our Bond* to both Frank Paice and the women missionaries attending the *Language Study School* in Calcutta, which until 1911 had been capital of India.

Florrie Cox also had the opportunity to learn Bengali, but it is not entirely clear what level of skill she attained.

Not everyone could cope with the difficult environment that would be experienced in rural India. Those who were able to physically and emotionally stand up to the hardships and stress could expect to be abroad for periods lasting for six to eight years between periods of home leave. Life was not just uncomfortable and sometimes hazardous in India, but missionaries could experience great loneliness, being aliens in a foreign land and often being rejected by both the local population and the British colonial masters.

It might be expected that India's colonial rulers would have regarded missionaries as "a good thing", but on the whole they did not. They often regarded them as "interfering do-gooders", stirring up trouble with the Muslim and Hindu communities who felt threatened by these European outsiders. Even those in the British Raj, who were reasonably sympathetic to the missionary work, looked down upon the missionaries in what was a class-ridden and caste-ridden society.

That said, missionaries did have comforts and help that were not generally available in their home countries. They often lived in large comfortable houses and usually were able to employ cheap labour to do all the cooking, cleaning, maintenance, gardening and other duties.

Servants would include a punkawallah – a man whose monotonous and unrewarding task was to operate an early type of ceiling fan to keep the missionaries cool in the many months of hot weather. As a further bonus for the missionaries, they could escape the severest of the hot weather by retreating to the cooler hill resorts in India.

As I have already made clear, my view is that missionaries were seriously misguided in their belief that "doing good" should be tied to seeking conversions to Christianity. The number of conversions proved to be quite small, considering the effort involved, and those who were converted often found themselves ostracised by their own families and communities.

Being a Christian convert often had a high social and emotional price attached. Most missionaries rationalised this with the Christian certainty that there could be no greater happiness and reward than to "take Jesus into your heart".

If life were tough, they could always cling to the belief that one day they would enter Heaven — "a better place" — as their reward.

4 A start to the jigsaw

I have already explained how the story of *God's Triangle* first came to my attention and how I first set out to throw some light on the truth. I will now move on to how the detail of the story unfolded. I will do that in chronological order, in the form of a diary, based on my emails, letters and notes written at the time. Put another way, I will reveal the story to you as it was revealed to me.

Melbourne — January 8, 1998

A visit to the Victorian State Library in Latrobe Street proves to be very fruitful. I find old copies of the *Nunawading Reporter* with stories about Frank Paice. One of these, dated August 31, 1951, reported his elevation to Mayor of Nunawading and confirmed what I had been told by the Nunawading Library archivist that Frank was part of the local government establishment in Melbourne. It also revealed that he was employed by Hume Limited.

These extracts from the article reveal a great deal about Frank's character and enormous energy:

Cllr. Paice has lived in the district over 25 years. By profession he is purchasing officer for Hume Steel Pty. Ltd. His interests are many and varied, but his close and constant attention to his duties as councillor and other activities of social advancement, leave him little time for hobbies. His encouragement of community road construction works is well known, and his latest enthusiastic sponsoring of the extension of the activities of the Good Neighbour Council to Nunawading has already borne fruit.

In this latter regard, the Mayor said in an interview, that one of the objects of his year of office was to establish the work of the Good Neighbour Council, which has now been started. This organization brings together all old established residents together with the 2000 new home builders in the city, and all the immigrants now arriving. Besides this, the G.N.C. is preparing for the reception of the 850 British migrants who are to be established in the city in eight months' time.

The Mayor continued by saying he wanted to see all new residents in the city getting settled in with normal amenities for living at reasonable cost, and, by the application of commonsense and co-operation, to work for the good of the whole community.

The article makes it clear that Frank is a very busy man indeed. Not only does he have his considerable duties with Hume Steel and local government, he is also a leading Freemason, an executive member of the Victorian Municipal Association, a branch vice-president of the Liberal Party, a member of the Blackburn Bowling Club and a member of the Mordialloc Motor Yacht Club.

As though all that is not enough to fill his days, the *Reporter* also tells its readers that Frank and son Paul have built "more than one" yacht and won several yachting trophies.

One very important part of his history is missing: no mention is made of Frank's years in India.

There is also a long article in the *Nunawading Reporter* of June 27, 1952, giving its account of the annual Mayoral Ball and the speech made by Frank Paice as Mayor. In this extract, Frank returns to his common theme, the need for a strong community spirit:

The council and staff had made it a very good year for himself and for the Mayoress, Cllr. Paice said.

Cllr. Paice concluded by saying how most present were representative of some organisation working for the common good, and how he would like to get the same individuals together on other occasions so that they might share each other's happiness and carry it away to convey it to the greater world outside.

The Mayor sat down amid applause. Mr. Charlesworth [town clerk] then rose to read a cable he had received from the secretary of the Purchasing Officers' Association in London congratulating the Mayor on the fact that having been the first chairman of the association in Australia, he was now chairman of the municipality, and expressing the association's pride in that fact.

The same article carries a reference to Olga. It is typical of the age that newspapers were chiefly interested in what women wore, rather than what they might say:

The Mayoress was a dignified figure in her distinguishing gown of iridescent grey satin cut on classical lines and featuring a Medici collar; a bouquet of cyclamen and daphne provided a bright note of contrast.

I smile at the description "dignified figure" and wonder if it is a journalistic euphemism for "aloof" and "unsmiling". (See page 20)

Finally, my searches produce a *Nunawading Reporter* article from the August 6, 1954, issue. It reports that Frank won't be standing in the next council elections and is retiring for unspecified "health reasons":

> Cllr. Paice is one of the longest serving councillors on the Nunawading City Council. He first entered the council of the Shire of Blackburn and Mitcham in 1935 and except for an interval of 18 months, has sat ever since. He had one term as President of the former shire and last year was Mayor of Nunawading.
>
> It is not as chairman on these two occasions that Cllr. Paice has made his greatest mark on the city of Nunawading, but over the years in the day by day business of the council as with his exceptional knowledge derived from a varied and wide experience both here in Australia and abroad, he has made a great and valuable contribution to local government in the city.

Interestingly, this article, while mentioning that Frank worked abroad, doesn't say that it was in India. To be fair, this omission may have little or no significance in this instance.

Despite Frank's poor health, he survived another 10 years before dying in May 1964, aged 75.

5 Some wedding fibs

Melbourne — January 9, 1998

Another inspection of the Baptist Foreign Mission files at the Auburn Baptist Church is revealing. There is evidence to support a rumour that Frank Paice's brother George and family suddenly moved interstate because of a family rift, a subject that I will have to investigate further.

More importantly, though, I find news of Frank and Florrie's wedding. The January 1915 issue of *Our Bond* reports that after her arrival in Calcutta in the previous November, Florrie Cox had made her first visit to the large Baptist mission station at Mymensingh:

> Miss Cox has been with us for a fortnight. She is making a spirited attack on Bengali, with good success. We are so glad to have her with us for this little while before the wedding.

> When she comes back to us as Mrs. Paice we will feel like old friends. We are doing our best to prime up the bride elect for December 22nd. Mrs. Lindeman took her to a Hindu wedding last week and I took her to see a Muhammadan wedding to-night. Miss Cox says that she is taking mental notes for guidance on the auspicious day.

Melbourne — January 11, 1998

As already recounted in Chapter 1, I visit Frank and Olga Paice's only child, their son Paul, in Blackburn. Although Paul seemed not to have been aware of his parents' missionary background when I first spoke to him on the telephone, he has since gone through some of the papers that he found when clearing out the family home after the death of his mother on New Year's Day in 1966.

Paul, who admits to not being very curious, had carefully stored the documents in his garage without having read them. Among these papers is a great find: a copy of the church magazine, *The Southern Baptist*, published in Melbourne and Adelaide in September 1912. (See page 18)

The magazine's front cover announces a farewell meeting at the Collins Street Baptist Church in Melbourne for probationary missionaries Frank Paice and Olga Johnston and returning missionaries Hedley Sutton and Miss C. Williams.

The magazine bears the initials W.G.P. That means that it was almost certainly owned by Frank's father, William George "Willie" Paice, and had somehow escaped the family purge of all documents relating to Frank and Olga's time as missionaries.

London — January 20, 1998

Back home again. Rumours of a rift that seems to have existed between Frank Paice and his brother George need to be explored. George and his family moved to South Australia, but I don't know when or where.

The date, in particular, is important as a means of supporting the view that the move was because of the scandal. Nor do I know when Frank and Florrie's marriage was formally ended, or when and where Frank married Olga. Establishing this has to be a priority.

London — January 21, 1998

I write to the Freedom of Information office in Collins Street, Melbourne, to seek some specific, basic information about Florrie's time in the Hospital for Mental Hygiene at Mont Park in Melbourne:

- When did she become a patient?
- Was she at the hospital voluntarily, or was she committed?
- What was the diagnosis at the time of her admission to the hospital?

London — January 28, 1998

It occurs to me that the India Office Library in London might have some useful information, as its extensive records cover the period when Florrie, Frank and Olga were in India.

As I begin scrolling through a microfilm record of civil marriages in Calcutta I strike gold almost immediately — the marriage of Frank and Olga in Calcutta just months after their return from Australia:

Registrar General of Births, Deaths and Marriages, Bengal
14 October 1919
Frank Ernest Paice, aged 31, Bachelor, Engineer
Address: 3 Aukland [should be Auckland] Square

Father's Name: William George Paice
and
Olga Alvina Johnston, aged 32, Spinster, no profession
Address: 10 Russell St   Father's name: Abraham Johnston
Married in the office of the Senior Marriage Registrar of Calcutta
Signed: F. E. Paice   A. Olga Johnston

It is interesting to note that Frank describes himself as a bachelor. I am told that this could suggest that his first marriage was annulled. Either that or he was just not telling the truth. Also interesting, and a little amusing, is the fact that Olga had lied about her age. She was 35, not 32, as she had claimed.

Even more fascinating is the official wedding notice dated September 23, 1919, claiming that Frank had lived at 3 Auckland Square for seven years, while Olga had been at 10 Russell Street for five years.

This was, of course, blatantly untrue. At best, they had lived at those addresses in Calcutta for just a few months. It can be assumed that if they had told the truth, they would have failed the residential requirements to get married.

As you will also see from the wedding record, Frank describes himself as an engineer, though he had not completed his training for this, while Olga says she has "no profession", suggesting that she had given up nursing after being dismissed from the missionary service.

London — January 31, 1998

In a letter to my family in Australia, I report the discovery of Frank and Olga's marriage, but express frustration that I cannot find any references to Frank's previous marriage being annulled or otherwise dissolved. I also tell the family that I am convinced that my Great Uncle Hedley Sutton must have known a great deal about what   happened.

London — Early February, 1998

A letter is received from the Freedom of Information Officer at the Department of Human Services in Melbourne stating that she will need approval from Florrie's next-of-kin before releasing any documents to me.

My mother, the oldest surviving member of the extended Cox family, gives that approval.

London — Late March, 1998

A brown envelope turns up in the mail from the Freedom of Information Officer at the Department of Human Services in Melbourne. It includes copies of three pages from Florrie's psychiatric file while she was at Mont Park Mental Hospital.

One of these documents is a *Request to Receive a Patient* signed by Florrie's elder brother, my grandfather, Arthur J. G. Cox, and dated December 3, 1948. It states that she is aged 61 and has been a voluntary boarder at Mont Park, but it does not say for how long. The document asserts that she is insane. There is a note added later saying that Florrie died of lobar pneumonia on June 7, 1950.

Two of the pages are medical certificates dated six days after her admission and signed by different doctors. Each declares Florrie to be insane. One states under the heading "Facts indicating insanity observed by myself":

> She [Florrie] has the delusion that there is a conspiracy against her. She likes being here [at Mont Park] but she does not like Dr (Cade?). Keeps asking for a cup of tea. Disorientated, confused and restless.

The other doctor, under the same heading, states:

> Patient stares vacantly, speaks hardly at all, gives no rational or relevant answers to questions but repeats such phrases as "I want my clothes". Out of touch with surroundings.

This doctor also quotes a nurse at Mont Park as telling him:

> ...patient has much deteriorated mentally in the last two or three years; is wet and dirty, restless and destructive.

Enclosed with these two documents is a photocopy of the inquest that was held after her death on June 7, 1950. Her death is attributed by the coroner, J. R. Burke, to lobar pneumonia, a form of pneumonia not usually associated with the developed world.

A doctor's deposition to the inquest stated:

> According to the records, Florence Martha Cox was admitted to Mental Hospital, Mont Park, on 16 October, 1945, as a voluntary boarder. She was certified as of unsound mind on 9 December, 1948, and was suffering from schizophrenia.

> Her physical health remained fairly good till 4 June, 1950, when she was found to have lobar pneumonia. She was treated for this, but did not improve and died at 9.10pm on 7 June, 1950.

6 Family memories of Florrie

London — April 2/3, 1998

I phone some of the Australian family members who knew Florrie Cox. Sadly, their memories were not of Florrie as a young woman, but of her life more than two decades after the divorce. By then, she was increasingly having mental problems.

First on the list to contact was Ray Cox, son of Florrie's brother, Charlie Cox:

I knew her reasonably well. She used to stay with my family from time to time. She was very difficult to manage, so members of the family would "share her around". I thought she was a little bit soft (mentally deficient). She had funny ideas about food and was a bit of a hypochondriac. She couldn't bring herself to do anything much. Yes, she was probably very depressed. I see her as a very soft, gentle person who just wanted to be a missionary and to help the poor natives in India.

Aunty Florrie had lots of mementos in the house. She used to talk about India a lot, but never mentioned her marriage. I didn't know she had been married until after World War Two when my father told me she had been married to a man called Paice.

I have a Missionary Society Cookbook with the inscription "F. M. Cox 1919".

Florrie's mother was very gentle, but she would have been impatient with Florrie, even though Florrie looked after her.

Next on the list was Norma Milne, daughter of Florrie's brother, Charlie Cox:

Aunty Florrie was a dear sweet old lady, but after India she was 'out of balance' and not well. She was very thin and had a diet that included grapefruit and bread that had been dried in the oven. What happened to Florrie [in India] was only talked about in hushed tones in the family.

Aunty Florrie had olive skin and dark eyes and could look like an Indian, though one of the family described her as being typically French in appearance.

She stayed very loving to the church and never resented it at all. She used to play the organ sometimes and would talk about Jesus as a wonderful friend. She didn't talk about what happened to her. I think she had blotted it out.

Her father was a big, tall man with a massive beard. Her mother was a lovely, gentle person and very religious. She used to say: "I love my husband and I love God".

Uncle Arthur [Florrie's brother, A. J. G. Cox] was a major in the army and behaved like one. He was very forceful and unloving. Aunty Florrie stayed with Uncle Arthur sometimes, but didn't get much love there. He would tell her: "If you don't pull your socks up, we will have to put you in a home". It was his doing, I think, that she was put in Mont Park Asylum.

Mum and Dad would visit Florrie every Saturday in Mont Park. She always looked very dignified with her hair pulled back. I always felt sorry for her.

Another one with pleasant memories of Florrie Cox was Eelin Hutchinson, twin daughter of Arthur J. G. Cox:

Aunty Florrie was tall, dark and beautiful with big black eyes. She was a very, very sweet personality and was very fond of us children. Her face always lit up when she met us.

Aunty Florrie taught in Sunday school, and we were intrigued as kids to see the name "Mrs Frank Paice" listed as a missionary on the board at the Kew Baptist Church, after we were told that was Aunty Florrie.

We weren't told what happened. People were very cagey about what went on. Our elders didn't tell us anything.

Grandma Cox [Florrie's mother] was partly responsible for Aunty Florrie going into Mont Park. They tried to keep Florrie hidden because she was an embarrassment, but I loved going to see her. I got on quite well with her and I really loved her.

Eelin didn't much care for Hedley Sutton:

Uncle Hedley knew a lot about what happened, but he covered it up. He felt it was a disgrace. He should have done more to support Aunty Florrie when she was on the mission field, but he had his own good name to protect. I always blame him for not doing more for her.

I don't think Aunty Elsie [Hedley's wife] helped. She was a peculiar woman; a very hard woman.

Another cause of Eelin's antipathy towards Hedley was that he apparently once saw her talking to a boy in the street. According to Eelin, Hedley prudishly disapproved of this and complained about it to her parents.

I raised the topic of Florrie with my mother, Rena Wood, twin sister of Eelin. She had little information about Florrie, but held strong views about Florrie's mother, Amelia Cox:

> I don't remember having much to do with Aunty Florrie, though there were all those stories about her marriage to a missionary in India. By the time she began to have mental problems, I was married and no longer living in Melbourne. But I do remember Grandma [Amelia] Cox. She was very, very religious and seemed to spend more time doing things for the church than looking after the family. There were complaints about this from the family. I didn't like her very much.

Ian Cox, the youngest child of Arthur J. G. Cox, had memories of his Aunty Florrie, but he was in his teens when she became mentally ill and at that age had other things to occupy his mind, rather than his rather strange aunty:

> I used to visit her in the asylum with Father. She was over six feet tall and one and a half inches wide. She looked like something out of Belsen [the Nazi concentration camp]. Customers in our newsagency [in Spotswood, Melbourne] used to take her down [cheat her]. Kids would tease her and call her by the nickname Sarah. It was considered very naughty for children to call an adult by a first name, even if it was the wrong one.
>
> Her mother was always going on about religion, but Aunty Florrie might not have been so bad if her mother had taken a tougher line with her after her return from India.

It is unclear how Ian Cox came to this last conclusion, as he wasn't born until seven years after Florrie came home from Bengal. But in any case, I have gained the impression that Florrie needed handling with more understanding.

Another of Arthur J. G. Cox's children, Bessie Carr, had these memories:

> Aunty Florrie was a tall, very willowy figure. I thought she was rather beautiful with her brown eyes and brown hair. She was a little bit slow and the paperboys at the Cox family newsagency used to make fun of her, but I thought she was rather lovely looking and very gentle.

Bessie was not surprised that no questions seem to have been raised about whether Florrie was capable of having children:

> Those things were not talked about in those days; not like they are now. Sexual matters were an absolute taboo subject.
>
> I remember Grandpa [Arthur] Cox and Grandma [Amelia] Cox – particularly Grandma. She was a very sweet, gentle lady. She was very religious. As kids, we

were not allowed to run around or play on a Sunday. We had to sit and read. If you were a Christian family you went to church at 11am, Sunday School at 3pm, then Christian Endeavour, then church again at night.

Bessie also remembered her Uncle Hedley Sutton:

He liked a bit of fun and would sit cross-legged on the floor and sing songs in the Indian language, but he was separated from the world — very austere, very formal and rather old fashioned. He would have been horrified about what happened [with Florrie, Frank Paice and Olga Johnston] and I think he would have handled it better if he were more a man of the world.

7 Two surprises

London — May 9, 1998

I report in a letter to the family in Australia that it now seems likely that the Baptist Church in Australia has destroyed all the key records concerning a scandal and probable annulment.

I also report that my wife Rosemary and I had sought help from the Anglo-Indian Historical Society at a genealogy fair in London. We were informed that even if the church had destroyed all its annulment records, there would still have needed to be a formal divorce granted somewhere and the most likely place for this was the High Court of Calcutta.

London — June 25, 1998

Another letter to my family in Australia passes on the news that Rosemary and I have been to the *Angus Library* in Oxford. This is where a great number of Baptist records from around the world are held.

We learn on arrival that it had an extensive, though sadly incomplete, file of old copies of *Our Bond*. Nonetheless, they contained a golden seam of information.

Rosemary reads through the February 1915 issue of *Our Bond* and discovers a report on Frank and Florrie's wedding and homecoming. It was here that we discover the surprising news that Olga Johnston was one of Florrie's bridesmaids:

ORANGE BLOSSOMS AND WEDDING BELLS

On the afternoon of Tuesday, December 22nd, a very select company assembled at the Baptist Church, Lower Circular Road, Calcutta, to witness the marriage of the Rev. Frank E. Paice with Miss Florence M. Cox, formerly of Melbourne, Victoria. The bridegroom, who has waited for two years with a varying amount of patience for the dawn of this happy day, arrived at the Church, so rumour says, quite a considerable time before the appointed hour. At last he was rewarded by the appearance of the bride who made a radiant and charming picture gowned simply and tastefully in white oeolian silk with embroidered veil and wreath of orange blossom, carrying a bridal bouquet of white roses and fern.

As the bride entered the Church on the arm of Mr A. P. Stockwell, the choir joined in the singing of a hymn. Two bridesmaids were in attendance – Miss Olga Johnston and Miss Mollie Upton (a niece of Mrs Stockwell, who is on a visit to India).

Rev. H. J. Sutton acted as best man and Rev. Harold Masters as groomsman. Rev. T. W. Norledge performed the ceremony and tied the knot firmly in a very short time. The bridal party left the church to the strains of Mendelssohn's wedding march.

Arrangements for the reception and wedding tea were carried out by Mrs. A. P. Stockwell at her residence, 6 Rawdon Street, where a very pleasant time was spent and the usual speeches made.

Special mention was made of the kindness of Mr. and Mrs. Stockwell from whose home Miss Cox was married, and who had done so much to make the day a happy one. Mr. and Mrs. Stockwell are both very well known in the church at Auburn, of which both the bride and bridegroom were members. Rev. H. J. Sutton and Miss Upton are also connected with that church.

The honeymoon was spent on the river, Mr. and Mrs. Paice going to which is to be their home, we hope for a considerable time. They received many dainty and useful gifts for their home and a good measure of hearty good wishes for a very happy, prosperous and useful future.

Home coming

Mr. and Mrs. Paice in due time arrived in Mymensingh, and then someone who had been otherwise engaged on the day of the wedding, met them at the train and waited till the luggage was despatched and the smiling couple were unsuspectingly seated in the gadi [horse-drawn carriage]. Then they got a shower of rice which had long been promised and were driven away uttering various threats.

We hope that they may be greatly used of God in the days to come, and that they may bring much blessing to India's people among whom they have come to work.

Knowing about Frank's long engagement to Florrie and his later marriage to Olga, it is difficult to appreciate exactly what to make of an observation in the wedding report that the bridegroom had waited for two years "with a varying amount of patience for the dawn of this happy day". Was it an entirely innocent observation? Or did the writer know, or suspect, something about Frank and Olga?

My research suggests that it was unlikely that Florrie and Olga knew each other before Florrie arrived in Calcutta, though they might have met socially in Melbourne before Olga and Frank sailed for Bengal. Florrie's agreement to have Olga as a bridesmaid seemed to have been entirely practical. Her own family and friends could not afford the time or the money to travel to Calcutta for the wedding, and in any case, the outbreak of the First World War would have made that difficult. Olga was one of a fairly small number of single women Baptist missionaries in the area at that time, so it was only natural that she would accept a bridesmaid role.

There was one link with Florrie's family in the official wedding party: The best man was senior missionary Hedley Sutton, whose sister Ethel was married to Florrie's brother Arthur.

As Rosemary and I work our way through the *Angus Library* files, there is another surprise: two years after Florrie arrived in Bengal she, Frank and Olga had shared a boating holiday in Kashmir and that Olga has written an enthusiastic account for the December 1916 issue of *Our Bond*.

It is clear from Olga's report that she initiated this holiday, which involved a long and arduous journey lasting several days in each direction. Was it just three good friends innocently going on a relaxing and richly-deserved holiday together? Or was it more than that?

Certainly, Frank and Florrie's marriage was not all it seemed, and it would be surprising if Olga did not realise this, being in such close proximity to the couple for an extended period. Was this holiday perhaps the start of Frank and Olga's relationship? Or did it already exist? We can only speculate about the answer, but two years later, Olga was back in Australia and her affair with Frank was becoming an embarrassment in missionary circles.

Here are some extracts from Olga's holiday report in *Our Bond*:

A HOLIDAY IN KASHMIR

During my first year in Calcutta I met a friend who talked constantly of the wonders and charms of Kashmir. Since then I have kept the thought in mind, and at last I enthused Mr. and Mrs. Paice, and we began as early as last Christmas to plan for our 1916 holiday.

Many have asked us about the trip, and it has been suggested that I give some account of our long journey to that out-of-the-way place. This is rather difficult, for space will not permit me to do anything like justice to the subject even were I able. Mrs. Paice and I took turns at housekeeping, week about, and we thoroughly enjoyed everything - even trying to speak Bengali to the servants who understood only Hindustani and Kashmiri.

The boats are beautifully clean and very convenient, being furnished with little pinewood almiras [cupboards] for clothes, crockery and stores.

The road is open to the public only on Tuesdays and Fridays, on which days the caravans pass and the road is guarded by British Indian troops.

The Hill tribes are treacherous and almost all are armed. At short intervals Block houses are so situated that they command a view down every ravine, from four to six soldiers in each.

Peshawar [now part of Pakistan] is a fine city, with broad white roads, massive buildings and good up-to-date shops. We were singularly fortunate with regard to the weather. We did not have a drop of rain all the time; only bright sunny days throughout — at first rather warm, but the last fortnight gloriously cold. Snows visible all day and every day.

As Rosemary and I progressed through the magazines and documents, we also came across this item reported in the September 1920 issue of *Our Bond*: the marriage of Hedley Sutton and Elsie Luke:

THE SUTTON-LUKE WEDDING

There was great excitement in Melbourne over the visit of the Prince of Wales to our city, but it scarcely surpassed the excitement and interest aroused in our denomination when, during the same week, the announcement was made of the engagement of our Mr. Sutton to Miss Elsie Luke of Jolimont [an inner suburb of Melbourne], who is so well known, and so highly esteemed by many of us.

The news of the engagement gave universal pleasure. Miss Luke has spared neither time nor strength in the service of the Mission. As Secretary of the B.W.M.U. [Baptist Women's Missionary Union] she has proved herself to be one of the most efficient workers on our Home Committee. Under her care the work has developed so largely that in most of our churches there is now a band of devoted women who pray and work for our Mission. But it is not her work so much as her own lovely personality, her generous sympathy and gracious courtesy that has endeared her to us all.

At this point, I should say something about the Sutton-Luke marriage, as Hedley's hesitant relationship with women may have had an unconstructive bearing on how he dealt with the *God's Triangle* crisis that emerged when he was a missionary.

It is safe to describe Hedley and Elsie's relationship as a meeting of minds, not of the body. My mother Rena was employed by them as a housekeeper in Melbourne in her early twenties.

Mum was immensely fond of both of them, but told me some years ago that she very much doubted that the marriage had ever been consummated. Certainly, she knew that they did not share a bed.

She felt that they were more friends than lovers. And because of Elsie's age, there was no question of her having children.

8 Two wars and Mymensingh

Melbourne — November 26, 1998

I return to the Baptist archives and most usefully scour copies of *Our Indian Field*, the official organ of the Australian Board of Baptist Foreign Mission. This magazine was launched just months after the outbreak of what became known as *The Great War*. Not surprisingly, the war exercised the minds of the missionaries, but for reasons that might not be immediately obvious.

Though *The Great War* (the First World War) is not specifically linked to the events of *God's Triangle*, it is worth reproducing some extracts from *Our Indian Field*. If nothing else, they give an additional sense of the atmosphere on the mission field and the priorities as seen by the missionaries.

Extracts from an article written by Hedley Sutton for the first issue of *Our Indian Field*, published in January 1915 show he is deeply worried that rival religions are using the war to try to undermine Christianity:

> Our papers are full of the war. Illiterate villagers stop us in the street and inquire how the "tussle" progresses. Anxious farmers dolefully quote the shrunken prices prevailing in the jute market. Retrenchment is the watchword of Government. A great deal, too, is being made of India's attitude to the Empire. Indian soldiers are to be employed in the fighting lines. India's young men are to have a place in the Ambulance Corps. Indian princes are putting their personal services, their money, and their men at the King-Emperor's disposal.

Hedley is particularly concerned about taunts that the war has "sealed the doom of Christianity":

> Christianity is fallen, they say; and the words are not the weeping of those who sorrow for the ruin of a great cause, but the triumphant gloating of men who are bold enough to plagiarise from Christ, yet weak enough to fall under the condemnation that light is come into the world, and they love darkness rather than the

light. The downfall of Christianity is not the regrettable murder of a helpful ally; it is the happy overthrow of a formidable foe. Yet "Love," says St. Paul, "is never glad when others go wrong".

Despite this, Hedley attempts to remain upbeat about Christianity's survival in India and is critical of the country's traditional religions:

Shall Hinduism prevail where Christianity has failed? That can never be. A religion that rests upon the caste-system as its base can hold no promise of universal peace! Shall we flood the West with Mohammedan missionaries in the hope that they may inaugurate the Reign of Peace?

When the Ethiopian can change his skin and the leopard his spots, then may Islam become God's Prophet of Peace! Shall we turn in our bewilderment to the Brahmans [high priestly Hindu class], and implore their aid? Somehow we find no substitute worth experimenting with.

The pessimism that our critics would arouse in our minds is preferable to the blank despair that would follow the adoption of any of the suggested substitutes.

Hedley is dismayed about the slaughter in the trenches, but continues to declare his faith in the "mysterious" workings of the Lord:

We admit as readily as anybody that we deplore this war. We confess that it is contrary to the mind of Christ that men should butcher one another. We pray that God's will throughout it may be done, to the uplift of mankind and the establishment of the reign of the King of Peace on the earth. Yet we believe that in His mysterious way God is working His purpose out, and that Christianity is not dead, because Christ is "alive for evermore".

The same issue of *Our Indian Field* has a report of the voyage in November 1914 by returning missionary Miss Edith King aboard the *Osterley* from Australia to Calcutta, accompanied by Florrie Cox and two other missionaries. She says their ship passed a convoy of more than 40 warships and troop carriers transporting Australian volunteers to fight for the British Empire. She expresses great pride:

On the way to the front: strong, brave, light hearted men, some of our best, prepared to give their all even to life itself, for their country. Twenty thousand volunteers, to fight for the honor of their King and country.

Edith King then goes on to accuse the British Empire of getting its priorities wrong. She points out that there are just four thousand missionaries in the whole of India "to fight for Christ and India's emancipation". She angrily asks:

Is this our best response? Is this all we can spare? Where are the volunteers for India? Great the need for our soldiers to proceed to the front, but greater, infinitely greater, the need for more men to proceed to the mission field. Great the honor to fight for King George, but greater, infinitely greater, the honor of fighting for Christ in India.

On a more positive note, the same issue of the magazine quotes from a cheerful letter written by Florrie on her arrival in Calcutta in November 1914:

It would do your hearts good at home to see us all together enjoying ourselves. We have had a splendid trip. We have travelled with lights out [because of the war], but have made the most of our time by learning from Miss Tuck and Miss King [returning missionaries] what we could of India.

We are looking forward with great expectations to seeing India. May God enable us to work there, and so carry out His command.

The February 7, 1915 issue of *Our Indian Field* briefly refers to the marriage of Frank and Florrie:

The marriage of the Rev. F. Paice to Miss F. Cox, late of Auburn Church, Victoria, was expected to take place on December 22nd at the residence of Mrs. Stockwell, Calcutta. After a few day's holiday, Mr. and Mrs. Paice were to begin their active missionary life at Mymensingh.

We have heard a whisper, in fact, several, that Miss Cox, by her brightness and Christian charm, won many friends, and congratulations extended to Mr. Paice were without reserve.

Then in the March issue of *Our Indian Field* there is a further reference:

Mr. Paice's wedding with Miss Cox passed off most smoothly and happily. Mr. and Mrs. Paice are now away on their honeymoon. They expect to arrive at Mymensingh before the New Year. A hearty welcome awaits them. We pray for abundant success to attend all their service for the Master.

It is instructive to learn a little about Mymensingh, which is 110 kilometres (65 miles) north of Dhaka, now the capital of Bangladesh, and to discover how thinly-spread the missionaries were. The small number of missionaries meant infrequent visits to some districts, resulting in a lack of continuity with their evangelising.

This article from *Our Indian Field* of May 1915 gives details of the main Baptist mission in Mymensingh. It also reveals that Frank and Florrie are, unexpectedly, to be moved to Faridpur:

Mymensingh is exactly in the middle of the district and is the centre of many activities. Miss Seymour superintends the Girls' Orphanage, where sixty or more girls are being carefully taught and trained. The Zenana [women's] and village work is undertaken by Mrs. Lindeman, Miss Williams, and Miss H. McLean, all of whom testify to the warm reception they get everywhere, and the deep interest evinced in their message.

Miss A. [Olga] Johnston is at present filling a gap in another needy station. Miss Lardner is in the language school, Calcutta.

The Boys' Hostel, which now shelters 21 boys, is in the able hands of Rev. H. J. Sutton, M.A. There are many indications that this is becoming a very valuable institution and one that will prove of great help in the future. Mr. Sutton finds his hands more than full with lectures, classes, preaching services and general super-vision of the work.

Owing to the sudden breakdown of Rev. J. Ings, Rev. F. E. Paice and Mrs. Paice will be stationed at Faridpur for the present, instead of at Mymensingh.

While the missionaries find conversions an uphill battle in many areas, *Our Indian Field* reports that their activities with the Garo tribe have been much more productive:

Under the splendid supervision of Mr. Nall, so ably assisted by Mrs. Nall and a strong band of fine, vigorous Indian Christians, the Garo [tribe] work has grown by leaps and bounds. The baptized members now number considerably over 1000, many of whom have been saved from unspeakable depths of degradation, but who shine as lights and are untiring in their efforts to win others.

Whatever my reservations about the motivation of the missionaries, it is impossible not to admire their intrepid nature as they cheerfully went about their work in remote, alien and sometimes-dangerous parts of the country. This upbeat report from *Our Indian Field* of June 1915 is just one example:

Miss Olga Johnston has had two months of itinerating with Miss [Constance] Williams. It was an invaluable experience to be associated with such a worker. She writes: "We travelled mostly by bicycle, doing fairly long trips. We had plenty of variety and heaps of fun, besides the encouragement of the work." During May Miss Johnston will be with Miss Tuck at Orakandi, and then will move on to assist Miss King at Rajbari.

The April 1915 issue of *Our Bond* carries an enthusiastic article by Constance Williams about the two months she and Olga spent tenting [camping] on their travels, which she described as "exceptionally enjoyable":

A number of the places we went to had never been visited by missionaries before. Almost without exception we were cordially, even eagerly, received. One learns not to place too much confidence on these first receptions, novelty counts for so much with the people; nevertheless, I enjoy that first glow of enthusiasm still.

Thank God, hope is our abiding possession, lasting as love itself, and in hope we rejoice. We had proof too, that hope putteth not to shame. In going back over old ground in some places, we found the welcome no less sincere, though less excited. If it is a joy to sow the seed, it is a yet greater joy to see signs of growth and to do a little to aid the growth.

In the July 1915 issue of *Our Indian Field*, Olga spoke of her struggle to get to grips with the Bengali language, and gave a spirited, more detailed, account of her travels with Constance Williams, including references to the cooks that travelled with them:

I am glad to be at work. I enjoyed my study at the Language School; still it is only now that we begin to grapple with the native language. I had two months tenting [camping] with Miss Williams. We visited new centres and old fields, and I was first in despair because I could not understand the language of the village people. It sounded like Italian, after the chaste Bengali of Mr. Page [their Bengali teacher].

We did most of our travelling by cycle, having tents and stores sent by bullock carts. How I enjoyed those trips! We had the jolliest fun and the most trying experience with cooks. Two were sent home with fever. After that we got a raw youth who could "boil water" and "make a fire". It did not sound too good, but we were determined to see the bright side.

Our first dinner hour arrived after a long day's work. We arrived home weary and rather cold (it was winter), and hoped for a nice dinner and a cosy evening. It came — the dinner I mean — cabbage, served in the pot in which it had been boiled, water and all; potatoes, likewise, and in their jackets. Another little plan of his I discovered one day, was to use the back of the knifeboard to slice and clean fish on. Needless to say, I took the innocent knifeboard promptly out of harm's way.

It ought to be said here that reports about the travels of the missionaries routinely imply that they did so unaccompanied. Not so. They usually travelled in a party that included several male servants and others who helped with the evangelising. The fact that the others were Indian and weren't considered worthy of a mention could easily be construed as a form of unconscious racism.

It seems clear from the travel reports that whatever happened later on to cause difficulties, Olga was enjoying at least this side of her missionary work, but as she later wrote in *Our Bond*, there were sometimes some uncomfortable situations. She gave this example of a visit to one village:

It seemed to us that the whole village had turned out to meet us, and also to inspect us. Why had we come? Whence had we come? How long would we stay?

We felt exactly like what I should imagine the beasts in a circus must do, only that we had no friendly cage into which we might retire. The garis [horse-drawn carriages] had not arrived with our baggage, and there was nothing to do but to sit down under a tree and be stared at. It seemed an age before the last tent peg was driven and we were able to retire behind the friendly bamboo blind, to the intense disappointment of the crowd without. Nothing so interesting had ever sat down in their midst before.

When Olga tried to talk privately to the women of the village, they were often interrupted by the men, who she described as "a perfect nuisance":

The women would just be comfortably settled in an interested circle when a wretched man, aglow with curiosity, would make his appearance in our midst, and lo, in a moment the women had fled. I would as politely as suited the circumstances invite the intruder to depart to some place where his presence would be more welcome than it was there. When he recovered from the shock this request gave him, he usually took himself off, but without being able to understand why we should have come to visit the women only.

9 Move to Faridpur and a crisis

Melbourne — November 26, 1998 (cont.)
The research continues at the Baptist archives…
After a few months in Mymensingh, Frank and Florrie move south
to Faridpur where Frank took up a temporary position as head of the
Baptist Mission Industrial School, replacing Mr Ings who had what was
described as an unspecified "breakdown".

A breakdown in modern terminology usually means being unable to
function because of mental illness, but back then the term could just as
easily have been used for physical sickness, such as being struck down
by a tropical disease.

It wasn't long before Frank began to make a positive impact, as this
extract from *Our Bond* of September 1915 explains:

> Rev. F. E. Paice has been interesting various Government officials in the Faridpur
> School with favourable results. The Inspector of Technical Schools has promised
> Rs.1,500 towards a new workshop and Rs.500 for tools besides a monthly grant
> for replacing broken and worn-out tools. The Inspector of Schools for the Dhaka
> Division also gave a very sympathetic report after visiting both Workshop and
> Educational Departments early in July.

The school had three prime purposes: 1) to teach craft skills —
mostly carpentry — to young Bengali boys, 2) to earn money from the
sale of products made by the students, and above all, 3) to convert as
many of the young boys as possible to Christianity.

During my research, I was given a copy of *Making Things and Men
in India,* a history of the school written in 1922 by the Rev. Lorraine
Barber, who made no bones about the third aspiration.

> We seek to bring boys under the spell of Christ, who only is the Way, the Truth
> and the Life, that such boys, Christ-possessed, may love and serve their school-
> fellows and their fellow men, even as Christ has loved and served.

Lorraine Barber did not seem to be unduly concerned about the serious consequences for students converting to Christianity. Any price to be paid was worth it, in his view:

If a young man becomes a Christian, he is of course outcast, outcasted from his home and his friends, and more urgent still is the need that he should be taught a trade and the duty and pride of being self-supporting.

Elsewhere in this booklet he admits:

Many [of the boys] go to Calcutta and seek work in Hindu and Mohamedan shops. Once there, they often have to endure much hardship and injustice, being blamed for all the sins, thieving, etc. of the other co-workers. There is needed somewhere in Calcutta a Christian hostel where these boys will have . . . a refuge from the unholy powers of evil in that city.

It can be assumed that Frank Paice held broadly the same views when he was in charge of the school.

Hedley Sutton also wrote of the difficulties encountered by converts. Here are extracts from a long article published in the October 1915 issue of *Our Indian Field* in which he shows contempt for the Muslims and Hindus and their hostility to any of their number turning to Christianity:

"...to win a soul, to bring will, love, reason into subjection to the obedience of Christ is a task of utmost difficulty.

How many outward barriers confine and thwart the new-born Christian? The physical hazard, no less than the social and the spiritual wrench, is beyond our words to tell.

To the true Hindu, anything, even the most abominable thing life can offer, is preferable to Christianity. Nor is it otherwise with Islam. Its gates open inwards to receive; they never swing outwards to relinquish. The Quran [Koran] places the sword of death outside the gates for those who will cross the line to Christ.

Yet souls are won. That is the gladdening fact. Those frowning walls, those unyielding gates cannot keep the house against the Stronger than All. But over-borne and spoiled, the strong man of Hinduism will attempt reprisals.

Hedley then goes on to recount how a Hindu widow "broke bounds" and came among the Christians:

In the town of Sherpur, where the widow lived with her uncle, there is a Christian nurse. She was moreover a witnessing Christian. Her light was not hid under the bushel of professional etiquette or worldly prudence. The nurse became a fast friend of the widow and in the end proved to be one of the living links uniting the widow to Christ. When the widow got away, Hindu anger turned against the nurse, as an aider and abettor in the escapade. Reprisals began. Stone-throwing on her roof at night opened the assault.

Then followed a social boycott. A silent sentence of ostracism was passed on her. Her every movement was watched most closely. Even the little children — little pitchers with big ears and ready tongues — were schooled in spying.

Hedley Sutton goes on to tell how the Christian nurse fled her home near Sherpur and rumours were circulated that she had been kidnapped:

Suspicion, hatred, a closer barring of the doors against the efforts of the missionaries followed on the winning of this one soul for Christ. "How hardly souls are won," when the price of victory is diminished opportunity!

We have reserved the name of a village not more than 30 miles from Sherpur. It is the headquarters of a wealthy landlord, a bigoted and fastidious Hindu. Report has it that the greater part of his day is spent in the ablutions and prostrations and recitations laid down in the Hindu's guide to the practice of religion.

To his honor, be it said, that his reputation for piety of the Hindu sort is matched by his good name as an upright man of business. But he is a Hindu of the Hindus, prejudiced to the very core of his being against all other religions.

Hedley's article then alleges other instances of bad behaviour by the rival religions, but tries to end on a positive note:

So success has its problems no less than failure. But through all the problems this abides sure — souls are being won, and souls are being built up and strengthened in the life of Christian service and endurance. And above it all we hear the Master's voice – "I know how hardly souls are wooed and won: My choicest wreaths are always wet with tears".

Hedley's article is just one of many in the missionary magazines that displayed an absolute certainty of the rightness of Christian evangelism, almost regardless of the consequences. Self-doubt never seemed to be an issue. Christianity was the only true route to salvation and must be promoted at whatever cost.

It must be asked how Lorraine Barber, Hedley Sutton and most of the other missionaries in India would have reacted if Muslim and Hindu proselytisers had responded by setting themselves up in Australia with the express intention of converting the entire local population to their religions? The answer to that question is very clear: they would have considered it an outrage.

To be fair, relations between missionaries and the local religions were not always hostile. In the March and April 1916 issues of *Our*

Indian Field, the editor, the Rev. J. C. Martin, wrote a total of 2,250 words of enthusiasm about a Hindu wedding that he and the Paices had been invited to in Faridpur.

He ended his article with these words:

> We left greatly pleased with our experience, especially with the courtesy and kindliness of our Indian hosts. With all the teaching of religion we give them, we can often learn from them lessons on manners and conduct that would make us much more attractive and, strange though it may be to say it — much more Christian.

Returning to Florrie and her plight, there must have been many times when she was desperately lonely in Faridpur, especially as her grasp of Bengali was still very basic.

There were very few Europeans in that area, and those who were there would not have been particularly interested in mixing with a missionary. Living in a large comfortable house with several servants would have been no compensation for the loneliness and the likelihood that the marriage was already in trouble.

To add to the problems, there was a crisis when Frank was stricken down by malaria, an often-fatal illness, particularly in that era. As reported in *Our Indian Field* of October 1915, Olga was sent to use her nursing skills to help him recover:

> Rev. F. E. Paice of Faridpur has been enjoying (in the technical sense of the word) a rather severe attack of fever, lasting about ten days, with a temperature varying from 101 to 103 degrees [Fahrenheit].

> The civil surgeon feared that Mr. Paice was in for something more virulent than malaria, but he fortunately escaped with the lesser sickness. Miss Johnston was able to go in from Rajbari and assist Mrs. Paice during what must have been a most anxious period for her.

This is particularly interesting, of course, because it once again brought Frank and Olga into intimate contact. Being a nurse and relatively worldly, any difficulties between Frank and Florrie would not have gone unnoticed by Olga.

Frank made a full recovery and in the May 1916 issue of *Our Bond* reflected on his first full year running the Faridpur school, appearing pleased with the way things were going:

> If I had the time over again I don't think I could have done more, nor would I have done differently. This latter remark of course is the outcome of a clearer understanding of the deep-rootedness of the faults in our own hearts, and in the hearts of those with whom we deal.

Frank confesses that the difficulty of balancing the finances of the school and its hostel is something that occupies a great deal of his time and thinking, "of daily moment" as he puts it:

I have had to furnish the hostel with beds, and with tables and lamp for the common room. Up to the present we have only had a small wall lamp and hurricane lantern. Boys cannot read under those circumstances. It cost me Rs. 60 last month for their books and stationery.

The School has a debt of Rs.300, but is more than financially sound. It is in a prosperous condition despite the fact that it is trying to help support eight boys for whom I receive nothing, and is paying wages to about ten more.

The stock in the place has increased to something near to satisfactory. I have bills to meet in the next three months but if I can't do it, I will pay interest.

Meanwhile, the same issue of the magazine reports that Olga is teaching at a village school she has reopened in the Mymensingh district. Though no details are given, the impression given is that the ultimate aim is for the students to become baptised Christians.

As I read through the magazines it strikes me that the life of a missionary seemed to be very serious. Certainly, the magazines didn't offer jokes or droll observations, and the only amusement to be found was unwitting. Take this gem from the report on the Australasian Baptist Missionaries Annual Convention in December 1915:

A KNOTTY QUESTION. Mr. Sutton read us a stimulating paper on "Missionary Institutional Work as compared with, or auxiliary to, Dispersive Evangelistic Work".

The loyal writer of this report no doubt thought it kind to refer to the lecture as "stimulating", but knowing something about Hedley's austere character, it would be highly unlikely that an audience would have broken down the doors in their enthusiasm to attend.

10 A bombshell

Melbourne — November 26, 1998 (cont.)

Research continues at the Baptist archives...

Frank wrote enthusiastically in the January 1917 issue of *Our Indian Field* about the holiday he took in Kashmir with Florrie and Olga. It was much less personal than Olga's account for *Our Bond* – surprisingly, there is no mention of either Florrie or Olga – but he does proudly reveal a past family link to India and makes very clear his enthusiasm for the British Empire and Britain's colonisation of the Indian sub-continent.

These extracts tell us a great deal about his character:

I am holidaying away up on the north-west frontier in the Valley of Kashmir. We came up through the Punjab — a land I have long wanted to see: a land where my grandfather gained his medal and five clasps for his five battles in the Second War. [The Second Sikh War, 1848-49, resulting in the Punjab being annexed by Britain.]

I have brought with me books, among others Colonel Durand's "Making of a Frontier" and A. E. Mason's "The Broken Road" — the latter title so suggestive of many a life. Both books, however, tell of how Britain has made and guards this same territory. Twenty years ago even the road over which we have come was only partly under construction. Now powerful motor cars travel it every day. We pass British troops every few miles...

Frank warms to his theme:

A British resident looks after British interests here. Kashmir is a free but dependent State. But if it were not for the road, both those troops on the frontier and the residents here would be helpless in these great Himalayan ranges. But there are roads further out still, and again further out into the passes of the Hindu Kush. Roads pushed forward by Englishmen at the cost of their own lives, by the score, and of the lives of coolies by the hundred.

We have passed the entrance to the road to Gilgit, of which Colonel Durand writes and there are ways also through the other passes, and they are fearful roads. In some places they are made of planks upheld by beams of wood thrust into the face of the cliff — the river roaring hundreds of feet below. It was by these that we have made Empire, and guarded it.

So then — road and telegraph lines and outposts of Empire, and men. All for an Empire. For six months of the year they were isolated by snow in their forts in the passes; sometimes besieged, as we all know, by the treacherous and hostile Frontiersmen. How easily, too, roads were broken. A boulder hurled from thousands of feet above, to crush through the planking of some part, or to smash up a column, and there would be no supplies available and the way back would be cut off.

The whole story is magnificent reading — the whole place alive with interest. The game has been great, and I am here and trying to enter into the spirit of it all as I rest and read and see, and think.

Though Frank recognises a need for the British Empire to crush its enemies in the First World War, he is convinced that the commitment to civilise and Christianise India must remain a high priority:

We too are "doing our bit" for Empire. We might be happier on another front [the war against Germany and its allies] for a while, but, like engineers of another army, we force the road through, or strengthen the road already made, amongst forces opposed to us on all sides.

These forces are natural and super natural, and how easily the road may be dashed away even from under the feet of the builder. "The Broken Road!" But if one engineer went down in the struggle, another took his place, and unceasingly the head of the way was drilled forward and went on, save for the momentary set-back of the triumph of the opposing forces.

We have all much to learn from the Broken Road. May God grant that we be used to make a highway, broad and wide, and safe and sure — a road for a triumphant entry for the Christ, over which He shall never be led to be crucified.

Some lives may be lost in the making. It is the cost of all such undertakings. Many feet may slip whilst the path is not sure, but we have faith in the end. It leads to an Empire safe and assured, and firmly established — wherein dwelleth peace and righteousness.

Back in Faridpur, Frank was impressing his superiors with his running of the industrial school, also known as the Faridpur Technical School.

Much of the March 1917 issue of *Our Indian Field* is taken up with items about the school. One article, *An Appealing Enterprise,* by the Rev. J. S. Martin, secretary of the Australian Board of Baptist Missions, is full of praise for Frank. He talks of the school's development from weaving training to carpentry and describes Frank's management of the school, initially on a temporary basis, as "a striking success".

> The Council had to face this situation: the technical school was growing in usefulness and was so highly appreciated that if the work were to be continued expansion was inevitable. Should we face the cost involved? It meant the possible withdrawal of a promising worker [Frank Paice] from direct evangelistic activity and the better equipment of the station.

> No question before the Council was more carefully deliberated. It was felt that from our stations many boys could and would be sent for such training. The new superintendent proved to be a born engineer, and had fine capacity for the trades mentioned.

The Rev. Martin then goes on to announce that Frank has been permanently appointed to Faridpur. He quotes from notes provided by Frank about the pressures he comes under to admit Hindus and "Musselmans" to the school, but also the impossibility of accepting all the Christians who apply:

> No one can feed them and I have no hostel to hold them. We are full to the doors and so full that these nights the boys sleep on the verandah. It is cooler [there], for the old building that had been turned into a hostel was once a preacher's house. It is dark and badly ventilated.

Frank's notes also mention that some of the applicants are put off by his firm rules that they must live at the school and must attend daily bible lessons.

In the same issue of *Our Indian Field*, an item headed *Home Notes* has further praise for Frank and forecasts that the school "bids fair to be among the most successful of our Australia-Indian enterprises". It appeals to Australian boys to raise money for the Faridpur school:

> Because it aims to give a technical training, principally by carpentering and cabinet making, to young Christian lads of our Australian [mission] stations, we have thought that the lads and young men of our schools could most fittingly be responsible for raising £79, the balance needed to build a new workshop. Australian boys may well stretch out hands across the seas to their less fortunate Indian brothers, whose country has been standing so nobly by the Homeland during the war.

The same issue of the magazine reports on recent Bengali-language exams for the missionaries. Reading between the lines, it appears that Florrie was finding the lessons a bit of a struggle:

The results of the December examination of probationers have just come to hand. They show that all have been commendably studious. Some, as usual, have found the acquisition of Bengali a severe test. Miss Janet Hogben has done notably well, securing first place in the first-class. Rev. W. L. Salter has done excellently, securing a second-class pass. The other candidates — Miss Burleigh, Rev. T. C. Kelly, and Mrs. F. E. Paice have all done creditably.

That aside, Florrie has an account for the same issue of *Our Indian Field* of how the missionaries intervened to help an Indian widow rescue her two sons from her husband's relatives:

She went to the missionaries in Brahmanbaria for help. They kept her and her boys on the mission compound for a time, but it was not safe to have them there long. Therefore, they were sent on to us. There was some difficulty, however, in getting them away, as the place was watched night and day.

But one night, it was arranged that they should leave. Just at the time appointed, some of the relatives came to the compound, with the pretense of hearing the Gospel. The preacher, however, was ready for them, and took them to his house, and read and talked with them for hours. In the meantime, another preacher had taken the mother and her two boys to a place on the river bank, where the mission motor boat was waiting for them.

They were concealed in the boat and taken down the river to a place where the steamer would call. Being safely placed on the steamer, they arrived at Faridpur without any further trouble.

Later in her article, Florrie has news of a convert:

Another of the boys who came here from Brahmanbaria 12 months ago is Morthur, a lad about 18 years of age. He has come now from the darkness and superstition of Hinduism into the light of Christ.

For some time he has been showing a desire to know more of God's Word and has spent much time in reading his Bible. He regularly attends the mid-week service and also came eagerly to the Bible-class which Mr. Paice held at night for those who were anxious to learn more.

Finally he came and wanted to know about baptism, expressing his desire to follow Christ in this way. After reading more and understanding what it would mean for him — the leaving of all the old superstitions and the living of a new life — his baptism was arranged for. So another of India's sons has been brought to find in Christ, the Way, the Truth, and the Light.

If Florrie were alive today I hope she would forgive me for smiling at the idea that the convert was leaving behind one set of superstitions, only to replace them with others.

As the months go by, *Our Indian Field* makes further favourable references to the Faridpur School, but the November 1918 issue has an announcement that would have been a surprise and a great shock:

> The Rev. F. E. Paice has resigned his charge of the Industrial work at Faridpur, and the Board has accepted his resignation. It is probable that he will shortly return to Australia. We have received a cable intimating that the Field Council will recommend the transfer of the Rev. Lorraine Barber to Faridpur.

In view of all the praise that had been lavished on Frank for his work at Faridpur, this must have been a bombshell for a great many people. It would have raised an enormous number of questions and generated potent gossip about why it had come about so abruptly — not least because there was no tribute in any form attached to the bald resignation statement.

A primary question must have been this: did it have anything to do with Olga Johnston? There is no mention of Florrie, though this could have been more to do with her being a missionary wife rather than a fully-fledged member of the mission staff. Even so, it would be reasonable to expect a mention of her, even if it were confined to something like "Mr and Mrs Paice will shortly return to Australia", rather than "he will return".

The following month the December 1918 issue of *Our Bond* follows up the resignation with a one-sentenced statement that is even less informative than *Our Indian Field*:

> Mr. Barber is settling in at Faridpur to succeed Mr. Paice in charge of the Industrial School – at least for a while.

That is, as far as I can tell, the last reference to Frank or Florrie in either missionary magazine. People of a curious nature would have had to resort to church gossip to try to learn what the resignation was all about.

11 Olga's eventful furlough

Melbourne – November 26, 1998 (cont.)

Research continues at the Baptist archives…

While I ponder the unexpected news of Frank's resignation, I switch my attention to Olga Johnston and other key characters in this story. Olga wrote a number of articles for the missionary magazines. For example, the April 1917 issue of *Our Indian Field* – about 18 months before Frank's resignation became public – devoted substantial space to Olga's frequently-lyrical account of the local celebrations of the Victorian Baptist Missionary Society jubilee. The following extracts demonstrate a powerful commitment to India, Christianity and the missionary cause:

> For many months we had been thinking of and planning for our jubilee. We have also been praying that during those special meetings we might gain fresh encouragement and inspiration, and that our Bengali Church might come to realise more of its responsibility. We wanted especially that our boys and girls in the school and in the hostel might come over the line and make the Great Decision [to become Christians].

> Some of us are still under the magic influence which India cast upon us on our first arrival. India is so beautiful, and beauty is God's handwriting and aids us in our worship and comprehension of the loving artist, who has painted such wonderful things in nature for us to enjoy. And the Bengalis are truly near to nature's heart. They utilise the simplest things in decoration, whereas we need so much when we go to decorate.

> A blaze of colour meets our eye. Purple, green, pink, red, white, orange, yellow, blue, heliotrope. Does it hurt your artistic taste, and does your mind shrink just a little as you think it rather loud? Perhaps one has to get used to it before one really thinks it beautiful. I tried to see it with the eyes of some of my home friends, but I am afraid I failed. Those colors in a sunset sky would only appeal to your sense of the beautiful, and so they seem to us. They harmonize perfectly.

Olga concludes her article with these rather complex sentences:

> Even now the half has not been told. Many of our boys and girls made decisions to

live closer to Jesus, though we feel that many raised their hands, scarcely realising the full meaning of the act; yet we hope to follow these meetings with others, which will help them to surrender all to Jesus, as so many of these old converts did years ago when they also were young in years.

The First World War continues to exercise the minds of the missionaries, particularly so as Florrie's two brothers, Arthur and Charlie, are fighting with the Australian Imperial Force on the Western Front. In the August 1917 issue of *Our Indian Field* Hedley Sutton reports that conscription has been introduced for British men in India and he indulges in some hand-wringing over whether the missionaries should be part of this:

These terms [for those to be conscripted] would seem to rope in all our missionaries, but a clause is added granting exemption to all regularly ordained ministers. It is thus open to us to claim exemption, and thus escape this military service.

The need, we all recognise, is acute. The more new men available for service within India, the more trained men can be freed for active work at the Front. This seems to be the purpose of the ordinance put in a nutshell. Loyalty to our Emperor and to the cause which he has espoused in this grim war beckons us to lend a hand to sweep away the curse that has hurled this tornado of savagery upon mankind.

Yet there is another loyalty — to our work as ministers of the Gospel; to the privilege of interpreting, as missionaries, our nation's ideals to those among whom we live and work — to those whose mouthpieces we are for proclaiming the Gospel. Anyone who has fought the matter out at home will know how to sympathise with us in our mental debate.

In the following month's issue of *Our Indian Field* there is news that Florrie is keeping herself occupied:

Letters from India tell of the busy life of Mrs. F. Paice at Faridpur – "she is in demand every hour of the day". In spite of constant work, Mrs. Paice was sitting for her Bengali examination in July. We all hope she will come through with flying colours, for she deserves to.

Then, *Our Indian Field* reports that Olga Johnston is returning home to Australia on leave [furlough] in September 1917. This appears to be routine, without any particular significance:

Late news from Mr. [Hedley] Sutton gives word that Miss Constance Williams and Miss Olga Johnston were expected to leave by the B.I. [British India] boat departing from Calcutta at the end of September. Miss Williams has fulfilled many years of devoted service in India. This will be the first furlough period of Miss Johnston, who was also esteemed on the field for her most efficient service.

Two months later, November 1917, *Our Indian Field* has news from home:

> Miss C. Williams and Miss O. Johnston arrived unheralded in Melbourne by the [British India steamer] *Gracchus*. They were heartily welcomed, and Miss Williams gave a delightful speech at the Victorian Assembly [of the Baptist Church].

At the same time, *Our Bond* has word of a holiday:

> FARIDPUR: Rev. F. E. & Mrs Paice — Mr. and Mrs. Paice left for Darjeeling on October 15 for their holiday. It takes some forethought and prearranging to leave a squad of irresponsibles behind for a month, but, barring fire and flood, and perhaps earthquake, our boys should take no harm, and we keep on praying they may do no harm at least till Mr. and Mrs. Paice return.

The December issue of *Our Indian Field* reports that Olga and Constance are taking a break of a few months before setting out on deputations, the word then used to describe missionary fund raising:

> Miss Constance Williams and Miss Olga Johnston are enjoying the opportunity for rest in Victoria. We have asked them not to undertake any missionary meetings for the present, and possibly about March or April the committee will draft a light deputation programme for them.

Meanwhile, the same issue reports that back in East Bengal everything seems to be going well for Frank:

> Good news from Faridpur and Mymensingh to hand. In the former place, four of the Institute boys are applying for baptism. This is very cheering to Mr. Paice in his arduous work there, and we rejoice with him.

> At a village named Shambagunge (Mymensingh district) where the work has recently been re-opened, four candidates are under instruction. The village has for years been the home of some professing Christians who bring dishonour to the name they bore. But since the Jubilee meetings held last January, a spirit of earnestness has been displayed among some, and the work is full of interest and hope.

Then in the February 1918 issue there is a brief note that Olga can be contacted through her sister and brother-in-law, Dora and Edwin Turner, in West Geelong, near Melbourne. *Our Indian Field* of April 1918 then has a further enthusiastic mention of Olga:

> The Victorian committee is planning a very interesting series of meetings in that State for Miss Constance Williams and Miss Olga Johnston, now on furlough. Something unique is promised in the way of missionary meetings, and information is now being sent on to the Victorian churches.

Another mention is made the following month, stressing how busy Olga and Constance Williams are raising money for missionary work.

> Furlough Arrangements:— During the coming months Misses Williams and Johnston will be busy in deputation service [fund raising] amongst the churches. At present Miss Williams is helping in Tasmania. During April Miss Johnston will still be touring in the Western and Wimmera districts. Both ladies will be in the metropolitan area during May, and in June Miss Williams continues at work in this area, whilst Miss Johnston will visit Gippsland and the Kerang and Northern districts. Friends are asked to remember these workers in their prayers.

There is yet more enthusiasm in the July 1918 issue of *Our Indian Field* for Olga and Constance's talks and fund raising:

> VICTORIAN NOTES.
> Deputation Work — Misses Williams and Johnston.
> During May the Misses Williams and Johnston have been conducting afternoon and evening meetings in the suburbs. At the afternoon meetings for women, Miss Williams has been the principal speaker, and in the evening Miss Johnston has given her lantern [slide] talk to a mixed audience, being assisted by Miss Williams. These meetings have been interesting and instructive.
>
> Some very interesting afternoons have been spent, when Miss Williams has related the stories of a "widow" and "a rescued woman" etc., illustrated by girls in the Bengali costumes; and Miss Johnston has impersonated a native teacher instructing some little girls, also in costume.
>
> During June, Miss Williams will be in Adelaide and Shepparton, and Miss Johnston will be having a busy time in some of our country districts. In July, evening meetings only will be held, conducted by Miss Johnston, with her lantern.

Olga's visit to Kerang in northern Victoria gets a special mention in *Our Indian Field* of August 3, 1918, but there is no more on her until the October issue includes a shock announcement in its report on the annual meetings of the Australian Board of Baptist Foreign Mission:

> During the meetings we received word that Miss Olga Johnston would not return to the field for "personal reasons". The Board has accepted the resignation and regrets the loss of a worker of such experience.

There is no clue as to what these "personal reasons" might be. However, the regrets expressed could suggest that Olga was not leaving under a cloud. It is interesting to note that the bald announcement of Frank's resignation had contained no such expression of regrets.

The board meeting that accepted Olga's resignation took place on August 21-23, 1918.

This is interesting because it helps narrow down the time when life for her, Frank and Florrie unravelled. As Olga's visit to Kerang was mentioned in the issue of *Our Indian Field* published at the beginning of August, it is reasonable to assume that there was some sort of crisis in early August or the preceding week or so.

There is another intriguing minute in the record of the board's meeting in August: "Resolved further that ladies going out to marry missionaries should be medically examined". Was it a coincidence that the board should have taken this decision at this particular time? I very much doubt it.

I am told by researcher Ros Gooden that all single women becoming missionaries had extensive medical examinations before taking up their duties, but it was an extraordinary fact that this did not apply to the missionary wives with their lower status.

It is difficult not to conclude that the board meeting had probably been made aware of embarrassing developments that might have been avoided if Florrie had undergone a full medical before departing from Melbourne to marry Frank. At this stage, it remains guesswork what a full medical would have revealed.

A search of *Our Bond* finds no reference to Olga's resignation. She had simply become a non-person in the eyes of that magazine. However, I do find some additional bland information in the Baptist Union of Victoria Handbook of 1919. It has this brief reference to Olga:

> Two of our lady missionaries spent the year on Furlough, viz., Miss C. Williams and Miss Johnston, both from Mymensingh. Both have rendered good service by deputation tours among the churches. Miss Williams has sailed for India for another term of service on the field. Miss Johnston recently resigned from the staff, and her resignation was accepted by the [Baptist Foreign Missions] Board.

I have also gained access to some of the board's minutes. Though cursory, they are revealing.

The record of the Field Committee Meeting held in Pubna, India, in May 1918 shows that Frank and Florrie Paice are still located at Faridpur. This suggests that the scandal has yet to break.

The minutes of an executive meeting of the Australian Baptist Foreign Mission in September 1918 demonstrate that there has been a crisis, involving what is described simply as "the unhappy event":

> Executive Meeting, September 12, 1918:
> REV. F. E. PAICE. A letter was received from the F.C. [Field Committee] containing Mr Paice's reply to the F.C.'s first letter, and the F.C.'s recommendation thereon.

The following resolution was passed -

That having reviewed the Correspondence of the F.C. re the resignation of the Rev. F. E. Paice, we express our profound sorrow at the unhappy event which has led to this action. We fervently hope that special grace be granted to Mr. and Mrs. Paice, so that in the future there may come to them something of peace and hope in the service of our Lord Jesus Christ. We recommend -

The confirmation of the acceptance of the resignation;

That passages be paid if taken to Australia;

That should Mr. Paice elect to leave India and not return to Australia, an equivalent to the passage to Australia be paid;

That allowance be paid for six months from date of resignation or three months from date of relinquishing work at the Station, provided that the Station work and accounts are left in satisfactory order, and that we await the arrival of Mr. and Mrs. Paice before this last claim is finalised, and if necessary modified.

MISS OLGA JOHNSTON. Resolved – That we confirm the decision of the Board re Miss Johnston, both relating to resignation and allowance.

The following CABLE to be sent to Mr Sutton – "Resignations accepted. Pay passages. Considering allowances."

The resolution passed at this meeting raises more questions than it answers. The use of the description "the unhappy event" particularly intrigues me. What could that be? It is also difficult to know what the executive's precise desires were when it expressed a hope that "special grace" be granted to Frank and Florrie. Did it hope that they would remain together?

It should be noted that there is no explicit linking of the departures of Frank and Olga from the missionary service. Indeed, it is possible, although probably unlikely, that the board was unaware of any connection.

A further meeting of the executive in November 1918 confirms that Lorraine Barber is to succeed Frank Paice at Faridpur. The minutes give no hint why Frank has been dismissed, or allowed to resign.

The minutes of the Field Council Meeting at Comilla, India, in December 1918 include this entry:

Min 629. In regard to the use of the word "dismissal" F.C. [Field Council] would point out that in the light of a specific representation made by F.C., Mr. Paice elected to resign. He resigned as a missionary of the Australian Board. F.C. would also point out to Miss Arnold and Mr. Salter that they feel the exceptional circumstances justified them as the Board's representative body on the field in dealing with the matter directly.

Again, nothing is revealed about how the scandal broke. The "exceptional circumstances" are not explained. Nor is there any clarification of why Miss Arnold and Mr Salter would appear to have lodged some sort of objection.

One thing the minutes do reveal, though, is that the meeting was attended by Hedley Sutton, thus confirming that he was aware of what had happened. It would be very likely that at some point he would have submitted a written report to the Baptist mission executive, but there is now no trace of it.

12 A court battle and a photo

Melbourne — November 27, 1998

First thing this morning is a visit to Carey Baptist Grammar School to see the very helpful husband and wife archivists, Ann and Alfred Mellor. Alfred is a former student of Hedley Sutton in his early days at the school. [Alfred died aged 95 on April 7, 2011.]

As already stated, Hedley was a person of some significance in establishing Carey and there is a substantial section of the school archives given over to his work.

The Mellors and I hunt through the archives for any reference to the Paices, but we find nothing. However, I am given a photocopy of Hedley's 60-page hand-written life story, sent to his wife-to-be, Elsie Luke. I don't have time to read it, but it does seem a curious document in that it appears to have been written entirely in the third person.

In the afternoon, I make another visit to Paul Paice, who has dug out his parents' surviving papers for me to inspect. We find nothing related to an extra-marital affair or their time in India. The nearest we come to any reference to Florrie Cox is the licence for Frank to get married in 1914. Curiously, she isn't mentioned by name. There is also one photograph of Frank in India.

Paul proudly shows me an obituary about his father from *Hume News*, a journal published by Hume Engineering and which had once been edited by Frank. This spoke of Frank being "a genial personality" and someone who was "highly respected by all who knew him".

It referred to "a life of service to the Hume Organisations and the public", but although giving a detailed list of his many interests and activities, there was not a hint that he had served six years as a missionary. I make a mental note to investigate this curious omission.

Paul also produces, again very proudly, a report in *Purchasing Magazine* that Frank had been elected a Life Member of the Australian

Purchasing Officers' Association as he approached his 70th birthday in 1958. He was described as "an inspiration" and spoken of as being held in "high regard and esteem" in the business community.

I ask Paul how he got on with his mother. He doesn't go into detail, but admits they didn't get on very well, especially after his father's death. She sounded a battleaxe, for want of a better description.

I mention in passing that my mother has given me a pin-fired revolver that Hedley Sutton had owned while in India. Paul surprises me by revealing that his mother also owned a gun in India. It was a silver revolver. He was told that she took it with her when she went outdoors in India and would shoot at the crows to let the natives know she was armed.

Paul says that when his mother came back to the safety of Australia she refused to hand in the gun and slept with it under her pillow for the rest of her life.

Melbourne — November 30, 1998

Today's main task is to visit the Victoria State Library to search through the microfilm of the Melbourne *Truth* newspaper for the report that was said by my mother to have been written about the break -up of the marriage of Florence and Frank Paice. The search covers the period between their return to Australia and when Frank remarried in Calcutta.

There is no reference to a divorce or a scandal involving the Paices. I also check the files of the now-defunct *Argus* newspaper, but again it produces nothing, either in its news pages or its detailed court lists.

I am deeply discouraged by the end of the day as the reputed report was at the heart of my research and something I had been building up to for about a year. That said, it isn't an entirely wasted day because a library assistant has urged me to contact the Supreme Court in Melbourne in the hope that its records contain something.

Melbourne — December 1, 1998

I start the day by phoning the office of the prothonotary (chief registrar) at the Supreme Court and am told that if I make a suitable written application and pay a fee of $37, they will, in due course, consider this application and make a search. When I explain that I am flying back to London in a few days, the court official readily agrees to make it a priority case. The application is promptly faxed to her, with a promise that I will pay the fee personally at her office later in the day.

On arrival at the Supreme Court mid-afternoon, I am thrilled to be told that the divorce record has been found. I am handed a certificate confirming the divorce and its date.

The certificate reveals that it was an annulment/divorce and was initiated by Frank. The decree nisi was granted on June 5, 1919, and became absolute on September 6 the same year. This is an astonishing revelation. How was it that the divorce went through so quickly in an age when there usually had to be a lengthy period of separation by the two parties?

I want to know more and I am told that if I make a further more detailed application explaining my connection with the parties and why I want the information, they might hand over a copy of the full court record. That is a definite "up" and I leave the court in high spirits.

Melbourne — December 2, 1998

Another astonishing discovery today. I visit a distant cousin, Warwick Du Ve, on a family history matter entirely unrelated to my research into the life of Florrie Cox. Warwick had promised me details of another distant cousin, the opera singer, Venezia Maria Rebecca Rangan, known professionally as Reba Rangan. Reba acquired a modest amount of fame internationally as a soprano in the early 1900s and was a pupil of Dame Nellie Melba.

After showing me his photographs and written files on Reba, Warwick produces a sepia postcard and says: "I don't know what this is, but written on the back is *Florence and Frank 1914*".

My excitement can hardly be contained as he hands me the postcard. And yes, it is a photograph of Florence Martha Cox and the Rev. Frank Ernest Paice at their wedding in Calcutta on December 22, 1914. It is ragged around the edges and has a nasty crack across it; otherwise it is clear enough to have been taken last week. I am gobsmacked, to say the least.

It is the only photograph I have ever seen of the wedding. All the others appear to have been destroyed after the marriage broke up. Presumably, this one came from the papers surviving from Reba Rangan's mother, Emily, who was Florrie's sister. I take copies of the photograph for my younger son, Niall, to restore using his skills with Photoshop. (see page 19)

Melbourne — December 3, 1998

Paul Paice provides me with copies of some of the photographs he has of his parents. In return, I give him a copy of the photograph of his father's wedding to Florrie Cox. He was fascinated to see it.

Melbourne — December 9, 1998

I transmit a fax to the Records Department at the Supreme Court seeking details of Frank and Florrie's divorce/annulment. In doing so I may have revealed too much for the success of my application:

The breakdown of the marriage was the subject of some scandal, involving as it did a missionary couple, and a search of Baptist records show that church officials made strenuous efforts to cover up the affair. Key documents were later deleted from the files. No record, for instance, appears to have been kept of the annulment proceedings that preceded the formal divorce.

Later in my application, I also tell the Records Department:

A number of my Cox ancestors were missionaries or otherwise heavily involved in church affairs, and I am anxious to get to the truth of Florence's divorce because of the several social issues that it raises. I am eventually hoping to write a book or article about the personal difficulties faced by Australian missionaries in India. However, as a result of the passage of time, no-one in the Cox or Paice families has any first-hand or definitive knowledge about the divorce.

London — Early January, 1999

A letter dated December 29, 1998, arrives from the prothonotary's office at the Supreme Court in Melbourne. It contains bad news:

Current legislature prevents the publication of any information relating to divorce records to persons other than the parties or their legal representatives. Unfortunately, after consideration by a Supreme Court Judge, your request for information has been denied.

This is a severe blow, but I vow to continue to pursue the matter, knowing that my application should have been given routine approval. What made this case different from others?

London — January 8, 1999

I try a slightly different tack. I write to the Chief Executive Office of the Supreme Court, appealing to him to reconsider the rejection. I make the following points:

...the original court proceedings were open to the public . . . and that it is inconsistent to retrospectively apply confidentiality to such a case. Additionally, I would point out that the case took place 80 years ago and that all the parties concerned died more than 30 years ago. However, the social and religious questions continue to be of considerable academic interest.

If you do not feel it is within your authority to review my application, I would be grateful if you could advise me what steps I would need to take to seek the information under the Freedom of Information Act.

Melbourne — January 21, 1999

My appeal to the Chief Executive Officer fails. The prothonotary's office replies to tell me:

> After further consideration your application has again been denied by a Judge of the Supreme Court of Victoria. It was determined that the court file does not reveal any information that will further assist you in the commission of a book or article about Australian missionaries in India.

This last sentence strikes me as odd. Very odd. How could the court know what information contained in the file would, or would not, help me with a book? Further, if the file were so lacking in useful information, why would a judge rule that it remain so firmly closed after all this time?

My suspicions and my determination to pursue the court file are reinforced by this rejection, but first I need to make a visit to Bangladesh to see what I can learn there about what happened to Florrie.

13 Exploring Mymensingh

Bangladesh — February 15, 1999

I am recovering from my jetlag and setting out today from Dhaka, capital of Bangladesh, on what I hope will be an informative trip to Mymensingh (see map on page 3).

Mymensingh is where Hedley Sutton spent most of his 20-plus years in India, where Olga was based for six years, and where Frank and Florrie were first stationed before moving to Faridpur. If I get nothing else from this trip, it will be a sense of what life was like back when Hedley, Frank, Florrie and Olga were there.

I make these notes in my diary:

The train for Mymensingh was described as an Inter-City Express. The image this induces rather fails to match the reality. The train looked as though it had been sitting unattended and unloved in a railway siding for several decades. Certainly, the carriages were built many decades ago. They had the appearance of the trains that used to run on Australia's railways in the 1940/50s, except that this one, with its 15 carriages, was being hauled by a large, relatively-modern diesel locomotive, rather than a steam engine.

As we rattled our way through the suburbs of Dhaka, there was kilometre upon kilometre of pathetic little shelters housing those at the bottom of the social heap in Bangladesh. It was dreadful. The shelters were each about the size of a small tent, not even high enough to stand up in. Yet, in these, whole families existed, somehow scratching out an existence. Some of the shelters were so close to the tracks that I felt as though I could reach out and touch them. When I asked someone what happened to the people during the monsoons, the simple reply was: "They get wet".

Chunks of my diary are not related to *God's Triangle*, so I jump forward to my arrival in Mymensingh:

An experience never to be forgotten. I was to be met by Beavan Peel, a Baptist aid worker, and when I had earlier asked on the phone from Dhaka how we would recognise each other, he just laughed and said "there'll be no difficulty because we'll be the only white people there". He was right. At least a thousand passengers must have poured off the train, joining the hundreds of people who were already there. The only problem was that I followed a group of passengers off the train, not onto the platform, but onto the tracks. Fortunately, Beavan's Bangladeshi assistant, Tarposh Mir, spotted me looking rather confused on the railway tracks.

Mymensingh station, though large and no doubt once quite impressive, was a dump and Beavan said many of the people milling about us actually lived on the station platform. Some had their cows with them.

The square outside the station was packed with bicycle rickshaws. Beavan and his assistant organised a couple to take us to his apartment via a few spots he thought might be interesting, such as the site of the old Baptist Reading Room and the local Baptist Church which was recently attacked with a fire bomb by Muslim extremists.

The big difference between Dhaka and Mymensingh was promptly apparent: there was hardly a motor vehicle to be seen. Instead, the streets were occupied by sedately-moving streams of bicycle rickshaws. The only sound was the soothing tinkling of their bells.

Mymensingh looked even more rundown than Dhaka. The Town Hall, for instance, was once a wonderful brick building from the age when the region was a British colony [and when Frank, Florrie, Olga and Hedley were there]. But it now was a ruin with plants growing out of every crevice.

We stopped by the Victoria Mission School for Girls. This was originally set up by the Baptist missionaries from Australia, but is now entirely staffed by Bangladeshis. Beavan introduced me to the headmistress, Miss Nath, who showed us about. There were around 450 pupils, all neatly dressed in blue and white uniforms. Miss Nath said she remembered her parents talking about Hedley Sutton. Our guide, Tarposh Mir, said his grandfather had been taught by Hedley.

Next, to Beavan's flat for lunch. This was in a very ordinary building, but was a real oasis inside, though I was told that it was incredibly hot in summer. One of the first things I noticed were low-voltage lights glowing in glass-fronted book cases. Beavan said the lights generated just enough drying heat to stop the books rotting in the high humidity.

We sat down with Beavan's wife, Marion, for a typical Bangladeshi meal of rice, vegetables and chicken, prepared by their cook. The meal was eaten in the traditional way, with the fingers of our right hand.

Beavan and Marion are from Launceston, Tasmania. They became aid workers after a visit to Asia and seeing all the poverty there. Once their children had grown up they joined the Australian Baptist Missionary Society and were sent to Bangladesh. Beavan was a microbiologist with the Tasmanian Agriculture Department. His main aid work is with Bengali women, helping them set up credit co-operatives, so that they don't have to rely on loan sharks for credit. He also advised on health matters.

One of his biggest tasks was to stop the practice of suspending toilets over dams or streams also used for washing and sometimes drinking. He said the health problems were enormous. Most of the surface water is polluted and/or disease ridden. Some time back, tube bores were sunk to draw clean drinking water from underground supplies, but this is causing the water table to drop, and in the process, a chemical reaction is now creating dangerously-high levels of arsenic.

When the monsoons come, a third or more of Bangladesh disappears under water. These annual floods are welcomed, provided they aren't exceptional, because it is the silt that makes the countryside agriculturally viable. The Bangladeshis put hardly anything back into the soil; everything is recycled in some form or other. The cows pats, for example, are all gathered up (by hand, I might add) and dried out or rolled around sticks of timber. This then becomes the fuel for the stoves. Even the leaves from the trees are swept up and used either for making paper or for burning. It is quite common to see old ladies sweeping up along the roadside for anything that can be used as fuel, or sold.

Marion teaches English to the locals. This is very popular, as English is considered very important by most educated Bangladeshis. Both Beavan and Marion are, in turn, learning Bengali and as a result, they can now have some direct communication with the poor.

Beavan and Marion enjoy their work, but they do find the isolation difficult to deal with at times. This is particularly the case with Marion, who cannot easily go out of the house alone, as she used to in Australia. She would be followed and stared at everywhere she went. She said she could drive, but this wouldn't be considered right by many of the locals. There are only nine westerners out of a population of about 800,000 in Mymensingh. Of these nine, there are just two women.

When Beavan and Marion first arrived in Bangladesh, they lived in a community outside Mymensingh and had no telephone and often no electricity. In Mymensingh, they at least have electricity most of the time, and more importantly, a phone and access to the Internet. They use email all the time and find this a wonderful thing to have. For other news of the outside world they listen to BBC World Service.

If you think they have it tough, spare a thought for Hedley Sutton and his fellow missionaries early this century. There was no radio, no electricity, no telephones, no air conditioning and no rickshaws — just the railway, a smattering of motorcars owned by the very rich, a few push bikes, bullock carts, boats, the occasional horse and gig, and lots of shoe leather. Communications were confined to telegrams transmitted by Morse code and letters that travelled by road or sea.

Additionally, they had to face all the terrible diseases endemic in the area without the protection of immunisation or anti-malarial drugs. Admittedly, there would have been a greater number of westerners, as the Indian sub-continent was still under British rule, but this must have been fairly modest consolation. The Baptists didn't get on well with their Roman Catholic rivals, and the British rulers were pretty indifferent – sometimes hostile – towards the missionaries, because their evangelism often caused trouble with the Muslim and Hindu religious leaders.

These days it is illegal in Bangladesh for missionary workers to seek conversions, and Marion and Beavan entirely agree with this. Beavan said some of the things done by the early missionaries in the name of Christianity were quite wrong. One example: converts from one of the main local tribes were forced to stop conversing in their own language and to speak only Bengali or English.

After lunch, Beavan and Tarposh took me on a further tour. As we rode about in our bicycle rickshaw, we saw lots of posters advertising the many political parties taking part in the coming elections. Because at least a third of the Bangladeshi population is illiterate, each party has a symbol, which is used on the voting paper. There was the Elephant Party, the Umbrella Party, the Chair Party, the Pineapple Party, the Fish Party, the Bicycle Party, etc. etc. There was even a Bucket Party. Heaven only knows how the politicians get across their policies to the country, though we did see several rickshaws getting about with loud speakers proclaiming the message.

The main part of the visit to Mymensingh was a tour of the Baptist compound. This is now much reduced in size from what it used to be, but still covers several hectares near the banks of the old Brahmaputra River.

The Baptist mission station is now run by Bangladeshi Christians, as Hedley Sutton had always worked towards. The building that housed the boys' school run by Hedley for so many years still stands, but is now a hostel and in rather a sad state. We visited the small up-stairs chapel, which is now a bedroom and study area for students. The former accommodation area for the missionaries and staff is also rather rundown. However, the Baptist Church building remains in good order and was being used for a community training session when we called.

A fair-sized section of the compound is used as a craft and re-cycling centre set up by Australian Baptists. There were a couple of open-sided workshops, mostly occupied by women. They were producing made-to-order paper from recycled newspapers and magazines, used clothing, and leaves from all sorts of plants. Other workers were making boxes and various other small items, while in another workshop, women were weaving various sorts of fabric. If I understood the situation correctly, the women were self-employed, so were paid most of the money from the orders. In another part of the compound, there was a training centre for disabled people, who get a particularly raw deal in Bengali society.

It was a very strange feeling visiting the compound after having read so much by, and about, Great Uncle Hedley. Just to think that this was his home for most of the first quarter of the century.

We returned to Mymensingh railway station a short time before the train's scheduled arrival time, but had a 45-minute wait. As Beavan and I stood chatting, a crowd gathered around and stared at us, as very young children sometimes do. There was no embarrassment on their part. If Beavan or I looked at them, they just continued to look back. When we laughed, some of the crowd would laugh also, though Beavan doubted that any could speak English and couldn't possibly know what the joke was. He said it was always like this when a westerner appeared. Some Bangladeshis have never seen a western foreigner, except in photos, films and on television. It didn't worry me. They weren't aggressive at all, just interested. But I did understand why Western women often found the attention so unsettling.

Beavan told me about two main worries they had in Mymensingh: One was getting good medical treatment; the other was what to do if they injured or killed a Bangladeshi with their car. Serious accidents are common on roads between towns – particularly involving buses and heavy trucks – and accidents inevitably attract large crowds. The assumption usually is that the driver of the bus or truck is at fault, and drivers have been known to be beaten to death on the spot. As a result, most drivers involved in accidents causing injury or death do "a runner" for their own safety. Beavan said that he would probably have to do the same. It was a terrible dilemma. Coincidentally, I was later reading a guide book on Bangladesh and it recommended quite strongly that drivers should keep going and report the accident to the police at a safe distance from the scene.

My train back to Dhaka arrived with the First Class carriage bursting with people, and it was quite a battle forcing my way inside. With the help of a couple of passengers I was able to "liberate" my allocated seat from an interloper.

The sun was getting low in the sky as we pulled away from Mymensingh. The families living alongside the railway tracks were resting and preparing the meals, while the children played just like children do around the world. There was one group with a wonderful, brightly-coloured kite high in the sky, while another lot were playing cricket with a bit of old timber for a bat and three crooked sticks for a wicket. Others were pulling and chasing each other and generally messing about, as kids do.

As darkness fell, the lights came on in the carriage, but they were so weak it was almost impossible to read. There wasn't a great deal to see outside, even when we stopped at a station. Electricity doesn't reach a lot of small communities, and even when it does, it is in such short supply that there are long blackouts. Beavan told me that a large part of Dhaka had to be blacked out one evening to allow a major sporting event to take place under lights in the main stadium.

Bangladesh — February 17, 1999

After my fascinating trip to Mymensingh, I had planned to go to the mission station at Faridpur to see where Frank and Florrie were stationed, but this proved to be impractical.

Although Faridpur is closer to Dhaka than Mymensingh, it is very isolated and the trip would have taken two days on ferries and over very rough and narrow roads. Reluctantly I cancelled it. Instead, a car and driver were organised to take me into the Narsingdi area, just north of Dhaka.

Over the next six hours I witnessed extraordinary scenes, some of them quite dreadful, some wonderful:

The most shocking scene was when we arrived at the bridge over the wide Meghna River. There, on the south bank of the river, I looked down on a vast dump of white rocks on which groups of people, adults and children, sat under black umbrellas breaking the rocks into aggregate for the construction of buildings and roads. There was no machinery, just chisels and hand-held hammers. White dust cast a shroud over everything around the site and would inevitably have been breathed in by the workers. I was told that the workers are paid by quantity, with the average daily income less than a dollar. It was truly terrible. A glimpse into the depths of hell.

A close second to this scene were the many brick works on the fringes of Dhaka. Clouds of red brick dust hung in the air, sometimes almost obscuring the workers from sight. What must this be doing to their lungs?

Because Bangladesh is constructed mostly on silt swept down from the hills over thousands of years, there is very little rock and the country relies heavily on bricks for road and building foundations. So, they make the bricks, then get people to break them up. This is work mainly done by women and children who squat for hours, at home or in small factories, breaking up bricks for a pittance.

On a more uplifting note, we came across a number of sari factories scattered about the countryside. The factories themselves were just ordinary buildings, but outside were row upon row of brightly-coloured saris drying in the sun. They made a wonderful picture.

At another spot, we saw hundreds of children lined up outside their school, doing their physical exercises. The boys and girls were in separate groups, each with different colour uniforms. We were up on a high road looking down on the scene. A couple of the teachers came up the bank to talk to me. They spoke excellent English and proudly asked me to come down to inspect the school. I would have liked to do so, but I knew that this would end up as a rather long visit, so I   complimented them on their work and politely declined their offer.

We saw many schools on our travels. Around lunch time, the roads were full of children walking along with their arms full of books. Though tens of millions of Bengalis remain illiterate, those who can go to school are anxious to do well. For them, education is a privilege, not a right, as in the developed countries.

On the way back to Dhaka, we travelled along a road lined on one side by communal ponds, each about 100 metres by 15 metres. The ponds are used to breed fish and to provide drinking and washing water, but they are also where all the waste from the communal toilet is dumped.

The toilets, such as they are, are usually a woven-bamboo screen around a small frame suspended on bamboo sticks, just out from the bank. The locals walk out along a pole, steadying themselves on another, higher pole. They then squat – and the excrement slides down the bank into the water. On several occasions, I saw people bathing and rinsing their mouths out in the traditional Muslim manner – all within 10 metres of the toilet. It was enough to turn the stomach.

Looking back over these notes, I wonder how much of what I witnessed would have changed from the early 1900s. The answer seems to be that it is mostly worse, and I felt that the trip had greatly enhanced my understanding of what life must have been like for Frank, Florrie, Olga and Hedley.

14 A living witness discovered

London — May 9, 1999

I telephone Mrs Annette Cameron, a prominent member of the Aberdeen Street Baptist Church in Geelong, Victoria. This church is where Olga Johnston almost certainly had her first contacts with Hedley Sutton when he made preaching and recruiting visits to Aberdeen Street.

Mrs Cameron has been through the church records and found this brief Minute, dated September 3, 1911:

> Miss Sherriff and Miss Johnstone [sic] having offered themselves and been accepted for work in India.

Mrs Cameron tells me that there is no further reference to Olga Johnston in the church minutes, which are complete. She expresses surprise that there is no mention of the bible that was presented to Olga in 1912 before she departed for Bengal.

London — May 10, 1999

Researcher Ros Gooden has been to Geelong to preach at Aberdeen Street and tells me that she also spoke to Mrs Cameron. Although it has been established that Olga was a regular worshipper at the church, there was no mention of her in the membership records. This might suggest that she was in Geelong temporarily for work or for study.

Among those in the congregation was the oldest surviving Baptist woman missionary, Elsie Watson. She had told Ros on a previous occasion that when she was departing by ship from Port Melbourne late in 1926 or early in 1927 to join her fiancé in Bengal, she had been approached by Florrie and asked "are you sure he loves you?"

It was undeniably an ill-judged and unkind question to pose to Elsie as she was about to set out for India to be married. It did, however, demonstrate that the breakup of Florrie's marriage to Frank Paice still hurt her deeply.

On this later meeting with Mrs Watson, Ros had hoped to get more information about her distressing exchange with Florrie, but by then her memory was too poor.

London — May, 1999

Ros Gooden learns that the Rev. Cyril Baldwin, a naval war hero and a former Baptist missionary in East Bengal, is still alive and living in a nursing home in Brisbane. She is sure that he knows what happened with Florrie Cox and writes to him seeking information. He is, by this time, more than 100 years old, but he replies promptly. He confirms that he does, indeed, know what happened, but he refuses to say what it was. Intriguingly, he says one of the women concerned in the affair was a second cousin. She couldn't be Florrie and I have been unable to find a link with Olga, so he must have been referring to someone else who played a less direct part.

Cyril wants the story to die with him, but I am sure that if I can get to talk to him, I will be able to learn more about it. Not surprisingly, for a person of his advanced years, he is quite deaf, so a telephone call is not practical. I vow to fly to Brisbane to see him next time I am in Australia.

London — September 15, 1999

I write to my family in Australia and report that Rosemary and I are making a determined, but unenthusiastic, effort to transcribe Hedley Sutton's hand-written life story, which in fact covers only the time up to his arrival in India in 1903.

I make this observation about the biography, written as a series of love letters during his long courtship of wife-to-be, Elsie Luke:

> Boy, are they boring and pompous! They are written in the third person and he [Hedley] comes across as totally self-absorbed and very, very pleased with himself. There are the occasional set-backs acknowledged, but for the remaining 99% of the time, he appears to have been brilliant, not just as a scholar but as a footballer.

> There are some further brief insights into his character when he accuses his father of refusing to praise his achievements and his mother of lacking enthusiasm for higher education.

> You would get the impression from the documents that Hedley was an only child. We are halfway through what is grandly titled *Hedley–His Story* and he hasn't

once mentioned his two brothers or nine sisters. Extraordinary. Well, I suppose he did say it was <u>his</u> story.

I just can't imagine that Hedley's biographical love letters could have done anything to excite Elsie's hormones - which may explain why he was 45 and she 49 before she got around to marrying him.

15 More Florrie and Mont Park

London — Early November, 1999

A tip-off from a contact who had worked in Melbourne's mental hospitals has suggested the strong possibility that the information given to me last year about Florrie's time in Mont Park Mental Hospital might not be complete. Consequently, I make a further application under the Freedom of Information Act.

Melbourne — November 18, 1999

I receive an email telling me that 11 more pages from Florrie's medical records have been released to me under the Freedom of Information Act. I immediately go into the Department of Human Resources (the Health Department, in plain English) to collect the documents. They are a goldmine of additional information.

The records state that Florrie was aged 33 when she first became mentally ill. This was about two years after her return to Australia following the breakdown of her marriage to Frank, but the records give the cause of her illness as "not known" – a rather remarkable statement, unless her history had not been revealed to the medical staff.

Florrie's condition was clearly not considered serious, as more than two decades passed before she became so ill that she became a voluntary patient in Mont Park on October 16, 1945. Not surprisingly, given her tragic circumstances, she had become very depressed.

The Mont Park admission records give her occupation as "clerical" and say Florrie is suffering from paraphinia. This is a psychiatric term no longer in use and I am unable to discover what it meant. The records give this summary of the information provided by her brothers, Arthur and Charles Cox:

Patient has always been quiet and religious, and never much interested in men. She was an enthusiastic Sunday School teacher but not morbidly religious. Her brothers describe her as "undersexed".

About 26 years ago she was married to a missionary, who, because she was unable to permit the consummation of the marriage, caused it to be annulled. She was depressed and has never been well since. She was "torpid", and would sit and gaze ahead of herself, and developed numerous complaints, thought she had gall-stones and diabetes, and arranged diets for herself.

For a while she worked in a newsagent's shop, but for 15 years she has lived with her mother and helped with housework, and then two years ago when her mother died, with one or other of her brothers, who are married. Lately she has done no housework at all.

Her sight has been failing. Since the onset of her trouble 26 years ago, she has had a morbid interest in deaths and illnesses, but little interest in anything else.

The Mont Park records then report that Florrie was seen the day after her admission by a psychiatrist, who made this report:

Middle aged woman wearing glasses who states that she has one younger and one older brother, with a sister older than any of them, as well as two deceased sisters, one of whom died of TB, and the other with a "leaky valve". All are, or were, married except herself, and even in her case she was, as her brothers indicated married, apparently in 1914.

She spent 1914-1919 in India, she and her husband both being missionaries. She has covered over the painful memory of her marital failure with what appear to be rationalisations, e.g., within two days of her marriage, another woman pushed her aside and said she would see that she was divorced so that the husband could marry her instead "so they put something in my medicine which took away my sight and stopped me having children. Before that a doctor had said my womb was infantile but that it might get better. They took steps to see that it couldn't by giving me stuff to take." She says that after the divorce in 1919 her husband married the other woman.

She believes that the divorce was granted because she was unable to have a baby, but she says that the marriage was actually consummated. She is not particularly depressed, but said she felt worse when her mother and father were alive, especially when she had the strain of business worries as well. Says her mother died six years ago and her father before that. She is apathetic. It is doubtful whether physiological treatment will help her at all.

There are five aspects of particular interest in these two reports:

1) The statement attributed to her brothers Arthur and Charlie that Florrie was "undersexed". (On what basis was this judgement

made? Was it a view arrived at over her lifetime, or since her marriage had broken down?)

2)   The reference to her having an "infantile womb". (What, precisely, was meant by this? How and when was this deduced?)

3)   Her assertion that the marriage had been consummated. (If this were true, how could the marriage be annulled?)

4)   The doctor's view that there was nothing medical that could be done to help her. (In other words, they appeared to be giving up on Florrie.)

5)   Her statement that she "felt worse when her mother and father were alive". (Why was this? Was it, perhaps, that they had no understanding of, or sympathy for, her circumstances?)

Two days later Florrie underwent a further psychiatric examination. This appears to have been conducted by another doctor as the hand writing is different:

> A peculiar personality. She seems to have woven into the actual story of her unfortunate matrimonial experiences a number of delusional ideas which, to her at least, seem to be the logical explanation of their causation. She is quite well orientated and no visionary defect is discovered. She states that in her younger days she was a missionary in India and while there married a fellow missionary.

> The marriage appears to have been a not happy one and after some years was dissolved. She believes that some people in India gave her some noxious substance to prevent her having a child. A woman was constantly throwing something into her eyes, "dreadful stuff". There was a conspiracy on the part of this woman and her friends to make mischief between her (the patient) and her husband.

> Later in life while in business [the Cox family newsagency] at Spotswood, a woman connected with her previous persecutors, also threw some harmful material into her eyes. There are no hallucinations of hearing admitted.

There seems to be a strong element of delusion in Florrie's account of what happened. It can be assumed that she is referring to Olga when making serious accusations about having been given "some noxious substance" to prevent her having a child and of throwing "dreadful stuff" in her eyes.

These accusations don't seem very plausible, though it is entirely possible that Olga did "make mischief" between Florrie and Frank.

About three years after admission as a "voluntary boarder", Florrie was certified as insane under the Mental Hygiene Acts. Again, the records state the cause of her illness as "unknown".

The hospital's Medical Superintendent, Grantley Alan Wright, made this note:

Diagnosis: Secondary Dementia. Prognosis: Poor. Mental and Physical Conditions: A voluntary patient at Mont Park for some time. Is now demented, out of touch with surroundings and unable to give any information about herself or help herself in any way. Is in poor physical condition, a bed case.

A *Request to Receive a Patient*, signed by Florrie's brother, Arthur Cox, a few days earlier had stated that Florrie was not suicidal, or destructive, or a danger to others.

Two Melbourne doctors – a Dr J. S. A. Rogers of South Caulfield and a Dr Evans of Armadale – signed documents on December 9, 1948, certifying that Florrie was insane. Dr Rogers wrote:

She has the delusion that there is a conspiracy against her. She likes being here, but she does not like Dr [Cade?]. Keeps asking for a cup of tea. Disorientated, confused and restless.

Dr Evans wrote:

Patient stares vacantly, speaks hardly at all, gives no rational or relevant answers to questions, but repeats such phrases as 'I want my clothes'. Out of touch with surroundings. "Eileen Lacey, nurse, Mental Hospital, Mont Park, says patient has much deteriorated mentally in last two or three years; is wet and dirty, restless, destructive.

It is difficult to establish with any certainty from Florrie's medical records what sort of treatment she received at Mont Park, but there is no indication that the doctors tried to establish the truth behind what they regarded as "delusions". Had they done so, they might have revised their views. Did anyone, for instance, look into her claim that she had an "infantile womb"? The records contain no references to any physical examinations, other than perhaps for her diabetes and poor eyesight.

Though Mont Park was built on large and pleasant parkland, life there was not easy when Florrie was a patient. The more difficult patients were in cages and living quarters were functional and often unclean. There were few activities intended to bring about a rehabilitation of the patients. Mental hospitals, usually referred to dismissively as "asylums", were in truth often used as a dumping ground by the medical profession. Consequently, the asylums were demoralising places for both patients and staff.

Melbourne — November 25, 1999

Before returning to London, I strike lucky again and track down a great niece of Olga Johnston. She is Marion Linehan, whose maiden name was Turner and who lives in Melbourne. She is a granddaughter of Dora Ann "Annie" Turner, Olga's eldest sister who lived for many years in Geelong with her husband, Frederick.

This is a vital link, as it goes some way to explaining how Olga came to be in Geelong, where she was recruited as a missionary.

Marion is frank and friendly and as a bonus, a keen genealogist. She is fascinated to learn what I have so far discovered and reveals that her family maintained contacts with Olga and Frank after they returned to Australia from India in 1924. This is particularly interesting and significant because I had been led to believe that Frank and Olga had severed contact with all other members of the family in their attempts to eradicate their missionary background.

While Marion knew that the Paices had been in India, she was not aware they had been missionaries. However, she assumed that her parents would have known.

Marion recalls that her parents, Harold and Thelma Turner, got on well with Frank and Olga, but neither she nor her husband, Terry, liked them. She describes them as "very dogmatic". She particularly disliked Olga and agrees with my suggestion that she was "a tough cookie".

Marion said it was the family view that Frank and Olga's only son, Paul, would not be allowed to marry so long as his mother remained alive. My researches indicate that this is probably true. Certainly, Paul's friendship with his wife, Lin, did not begin until after Olga died on New Year's Day, 1966.

London — December 30, 1999

A doctor friend, Albert Goonetilleke, thinks that Florrie's condition was probably the result of a chromosome mix-up. He reckons that she was probably a boy who failed to develop properly in the womb. But he doesn't claim to be an expert in that field and is unable to precisely identify the condition.

16 More on Frank and Olga

London — January 27, 2000

Paul and Lin Paice are visiting the UK and Ireland. We have a long chat on the telephone, but are not able to meet face-to-face.

I ask Paul if he is interested in what I am discovering during my researches, and he says he is. He would have liked to have done it himself, but was "probably too lazy". His words seem genuine enough. He says he has carefully kept all the documents I have sent him.

I tell him about the doctor friend, supporting my suspicions that Florrie's condition was probably the result of a chromosome mix-up, and we discuss the shock that Paul's father might have suffered on discovering such a condition, even if that condition was not fully understood at the time.

I also tell Paul that I had discovered an entry by his father in the autograph book of Maude Irene "Rena" Sutton, sister of Hedley Sutton. This was dated in 1910, about 13 months before she died from TB. We speculated, without coming to any conclusion, whether Frank might have been a close friend of Rena Sutton, before becoming friendly with Florrie. I explain that the connection may have been no more than the fact that Frank, the Coxes and the Suttons all went to the Auburn Baptist Church, though I understood it to have been unusual back then for a single man to make an entry in a single woman's autograph book, unless there was a close friendship.

I also inform Paul of my discovery that his German-born grandmother Julia was just 17 when she married Abraham Johnston, who was 38. When I tell him that Julia had died aged 37, about four years after the birth of Olga, he recalls his mother saying that she had been brought up by her father and her older sister, Annie (Dora Anna Turner, née Johnston), who lived in Geelong for a long while.

Paul gives me information about his Paice grandfather, William George "Willie" Paice. He describes him as a "sky pilot", which he explains was someone who was very religious but not actually an ordained minister.

He says his grandfather inspired both his sons, Frank and George, to become ministers. His grandfather lived at 32 Fuschia Street, Blackburn. Paul says his father then bought numbers 28 and 30 and built his house on 28. Number 30 was later sold and now has a house on it.

Paul again tells me that his father talked very little about his marriage to Florrie Cox, and didn't know until after he married Florrie that she couldn't have children. He confirms that Olga also had difficulties with pregnancies. Her first two pregnancies failed, though he wasn't sure whether they were miscarriages or stillbirths.

It is again clear that Paul hero-worshipped his father, but not so his mother. I suggest to Paul that his mother was a very complex woman. He described her as open. "Blunt?", I asked. No, he said, but she came straight out with things. He said business people used to thank her for "bringing things that weren't right to their attention". I suspect that Paul is just being polite about his mother.

Somehow — I'm not quite sure how — we got onto the subject of which hand was normally used for writing. I mention that I am left-handed by instinct, but that in my final year of primary school, I had been forced to switch to writing with my right hand. Paul said the opposite had happened with his mother; her teacher had made her switch from right to left hand, but after leaving school she had switched back again. He said his mother had a "fixation" about people who wrote with their left hands. He was unable to explain this fixation, but it was clear that she didn't like left-handed people. One possibility could be the South Asian practice of using the left hand to wipe or wash themselves after visiting the toilet.

Reflecting on this and previous conversations with Paul about his mother, I am now confident that I understand the essence of Olga's character reasonably accurately.

17 The court battle resumes

London — March 3, 2000

Time to return to my attempts to have the Supreme Court in Melbourne hand over more information about the annulment of Frank and Florrie's marriage.

At Paul Paice's request, I draft a letter for him to submit to the court, pointing out that both of the parties to the annulment are now deceased.

Melbourne — March 29, 2000

The court writes back to Paul, telling him that he should make a more detailed application, so that this can be considered by a judge.

London — April 17, 2000

Paul writes back to the Supreme Court with the requested details and adds:

> While I was made aware by my father that he had been married before, I was given no details, except that the marriage was annulled by the Baptist Church for reasons that are not clear. I am anxious to know the cause of the breakdown of the first marriage.

London — May 24, 2000

Paul Paice telephones me from Melbourne. He was in an agitated state, wondering why I seemed to be in such a rush to get the result of his application to the Supreme Court for details of his father's divorce. He wondered whether I had another purpose and was going to be nasty about his father.

This seems to have been triggered by a call I made to him yesterday. He was not available and the call had been taken by wife Lin who passed on a message that I had called. I assume Paul felt harassed.

I explain that I phoned because my emails to him had gone unanswered. As he was new to using emails, I feared he had not received them. Paul admits that he has been having trouble getting the hang of emails. He hadn't realised that it was the usual practice to reply to them promptly, rather than put them aside like a letter, to be answered in due course. He says his son in London had also complained to him about ignoring emails.

Paul is assured that I am not trying "to do down" his father, but am keenly interested in finding out what happened to his parents, Frank and Olga, on a personal level. I remind him again that I was also working on a film script based on the story of what happened to my great aunt and his father. I repeat that it is my intention to change all the names. In any case, I feel that his father comes out of my enquiries quite well. I add, though, that his mother's character hasn't come out quite so well.

Paul seems satisfied by what I tell him and the rest of the conversation is very friendly. He tells me that his application to the Supreme Court has been rejected. He is annoyed at not being able to get the information and phoned the court to ask why. He says that the court official seemed to be telling him that what his parents had done was considered "illegal" at the time. I ask Paul if the word was bigamy. He says no, but he can't remember the word the court official used. (I think it was probably co-habiting.) The court official promised to phone him back later that day with more information, but had not. Paul promises to try to contact the official again.

Paul Paice's phone call gets me wondering what is going on at the Supreme Court. I make the following note:

> I am becoming increasingly suspicious about this. First of all, how was it that such a controversial case never got into the newspapers in an age when divorce cases were usually reported in lip-smacking detail in the *Argus* and Melbourne *Truth*? And why does the court refuse so resolutely to make the papers public to members of the two families involved when the original hearing would have been held in public? Or was it? I wonder if the case might have been held *in camera* because it was so sensitive?

> The infuriating thing is that if the divorce had been dealt with just two years earlier (i.e. in 1917), the documents would probably be available for all to see at Melbourne's Public Records Office, along with every other divorce file for that period. I ponder again whether it might be possible to gain access to the files through the Freedom of Information Act.

London — July 22, 2000

I write a letter to the Freedom of Information Office at the Supreme Court, hoping for some clarification. I make the following points:

Both myself (a great nephew of Florence M. Paice) and Paul Paice (only child of Frank E. Paice) have applied over the past two years for access to these files. Our applications have been refused, even though all the parties concerned are long dead.

The divorce hearing took place in 1919, and I understand this followed the granting of an annulment by the Baptist Church of Australia.

I further understand that divorce hearings were normally open to the public and, indeed, were usually reported in great detail in the newspapers of the day. Yet the Paice divorce case was never mentioned in the newspapers, either in the news columns or in the court lists.

I find it curious that such a controversial divorce case – involving as it did, a group of Australian missionaries – wasn't reported in the press. I find it even more curious that 80 years on, there appears to be a retrospective ban on information about the case being made public. After all, if the case had been heard just 18 months earlier, the files would now be at the PRO and open to anyone to view.

The impression both Mr Paice and myself gained when making our applications was that it would be a relatively routine matter. I have also consulted lawyer friends in Melbourne, and they have expressed surprise that the court has refused to give us any information.

Therefore, I would be grateful if you could provide the answers to the following questions:

1) Was the divorce hearing held in an open court?

2) Was any form of ban on publicity imposed by the court at the time?

3) Are there any plans to hand over divorce court records later than 1917 to the PRO office?

4) If so, will the Paice papers be among them?

Yours sincerely, Ian Richardson

Melbourne — August 4, 2000

Paul Paice emails me with the news that he finally managed to talk to someone at the Supreme Court and had been told that the requested file wasn't currently available because of an office move. He is told that there may be a three-week wait.

London — August 24, 2000

Still no response from the Supreme Court and I express a view to my family that the "office move" may be just an excuse.

London — September 27, 2000

In a note to my family, I tell them that further research into Great Aunt Florrie's condition suggests that she could have had Kleinfelter's XXY Syndrome. If this were so, Florrie would have actually been male.

London — September 28, 2000

The Registry Officer of the Supreme Court, Paul O'Halloran, emails me as a follow-up to a telephone call in which he had told me that my letter of July 22 had been "passed about" by the court.

The official told me that under the present legislation the divorce documents would "never be released to the public". He expressed the view that the divorce hearing would have been in open court. I told him I thought there had been a cover-up.

Today's email tells me that in the light of the phone conversation, the prothonotary had now requested to see the file which lies in a warehouse outside the court. This would take about six days, after which the prothonotary would consider my letter of July 22.

London — September 30, 2000

I receive an email from Paul Paice informing me that he has also been trying to get some answers from the Supreme Court. He, too, was told that the divorce file would never be released, but after an argument over the telephone, Paul was told that the matter would be referred to the prothonotary.

London — October 30, 2000

Frustration is getting the better of me and I phone Paul O'Halloran to try to establish why the court still hadn't contacted me about the July 22 letter. He explains that he has been away on leave. While we chat he goes through his InTray and finds that the file has turned up in his absence and been dealt with by the prothonotary.

He tells me that the prothonotary had expressed the view that it "appeared" that the divorce hearing took place in open court, and it "appeared" that there was no ban on publicity (i.e. there was no Suppression Order). The prothonotary said the papers were closed to the public and always would be.

Paul O'Halloran explains that because of the "sensitive nature" of the file, the court would not be prepared to release them. When I asked him to explain what he meant by "sensitive nature", he said he guessed that any revelations about my great aunt's gender would have been viewed as "quite shocking".

His reference to Florrie Cox's gender made it sound as though the officer had gained this information from reading the file. However, it is possible that he was simply picking up on my statement earlier in the conversation that I was reasonably sure that she was part man/part woman.

I felt that I couldn't press him further on this for fear of causing him to clam up. He had been friendly throughout this and previous conversations, and I was left with the impression that he was being as helpful as he could without breaking the prothonotary's ruling.

As we concluded our conversation, I thanked him for his help and said that I would probably now seek professional legal advice to further my case. He said that he doubted this would be successful because there was no appeal body.

London — October 31, 2000

I receive an email from the Supreme Court. A letter from Paul O'Halloran is attached, confirming our telephone conversation:

- It appears from the documents contained on the court file that the hearing was held in open court, as was the procedure for divorce matters. No document on the file indicates the hearing was <u>not</u> held in open court.

- No document on the court file mentions any ban on publicity.

- There are no plans to enable public access to divorce files held by the Supreme Court of Victoria. All court divorce files are confidential and will continue to be so.

So, another setback for me. It does, again, raise a serious question: If the hearing was in open court with no ban on publicity, why did it not get the sort of press coverage that juicy divorce cases normally received in newspapers such as the Melbourne *Truth* and Melbourne *Argus*? Was there some sort of conspiracy – say, between the Baptist Church and the newspapers – to ignore the hearing?

A further question: Why was this case alone marked "closed for all time" if the initial hearing was in an open court?

Melbourne — November 20, 2000

Back in Australia, I talk to Ron Winsall, the best man at my wedding and a former superintendent in the Victoria State Police.

He thinks it extraordinary that I hadn't been able to get access to the divorce papers and he urges me to contact the Administrative Appeals Tribunal, which deals with a whole range of Freedom of Information Act matters. He advises me to be clear about whether my application to the Supreme Court has already been processed through the Freedom of Information Act.

I phone Paul O'Halloran to ask him about Freedom of Information applications to the court. He explains that the court does not have an FoI officer and Freedom of Information applications always go to the prothonotary's office for processing.

Paul seems sympathetic, but it is not down to him to agree to release the file. He suggests the best course of action is to have a meeting with the-then prothonotary, Joe Saltalamacchia, to put my case face-to-face.

Melbourne — November 23, 2000

An agreeable, but not very helpful, meeting takes place with Joe Saltalamacchia at the Supreme Court. I put my case as best I can, but he is not optimistic that I can get the "closed for all time" ruling overturned. He confirms that a judge recently reaffirmed that the papers should not be released for inspection by descendants of the parties concerned, or by members of the public.

He cannot be persuaded to tell me anything about what the file contains. All he will do is confirm that the original hearing appeared to have been held in open court and that there was no suggestion of a suppression order. He is unable to offer any thoughts on how the divorce was kept out of the newspapers.

We parted on friendly terms with my making it clear that I was even more determined than ever to continue my battle to gain access to the divorce file.

18 Victory at last

London — January 29, 2001

Back home and increasingly frustrated by my lack of progress with the Supreme Court, I take up an offer of advice from my Uncle Ian Cox's partner, Rosemary Varty, who was a Cabinet member in the Victorian State Government during Jeff Kennett's term as Premier.

I supply a two-page briefing paper for Rosemary, telling her what I have so far been able to establish or surmise. I express my bafflement at why, and how, the scandal was so well covered up:

> Despite the sensational nature of the events, the church successfully kept the scandal within a small group of family members and church officials. In my considered opinion, the only viable conclusion to be drawn is that the Supreme Court judge who presided over the divorce hearing played a role in this.

> Over the past two years I have consulted a number of legal people in Melbourne about this matter and they have universally expressed surprise that these court papers have been retrospectively made confidential.

> They also cannot think of any justification for a contemporary Supreme Court judge to order the suppression of events that took place so long ago and where the only child of either marriage is a party to the application.

London — March 31, 2001

In a letter to my family, I report that I have discussed the case with the Rev. Geoffrey Rowse, my wife's cousin who is a District Superintendent with the Baptist Church in Melbourne.

He tells me that he has never heard of a marriage annulment by the Baptists. My researcher, Ros Gooden, has also not been able to find anyone in the church who knows of an annulment.

The conclusion to draw from this is that the annulment granted in the Supreme Court of Victoria on June 5, 1919 was a strictly-judicial affair and probably nothing to do with the church.

London — April 5, 2001

An email arrives from Ros Gooden, answering my request for a list of members of the Victorian Baptist Mission Society in 1918 when the scandal surrounding Frank, Florrie and Olga first broke.

The members include Elsie Luke, who was later to marry Hedley Sutton. More importantly, the chairman was Joseph H. Goble, a high-profile and distinguished Baptist preacher and Freemason.

Although the Baptists didn't particularly approve of Freemasonry, Pastor Goble was a member of the Footscray St John's Lodge No. 71 for some years. This is a further piece of the jigsaw in that it supports my suspicions that the Freemasons played a major role in covering up the scandal.

London — May 3, 2001

An email arrives from Paul Paice confirming that his father was a Freemason. He reports that Frank joined a lodge in Blackburn in 1928 and later the Victoria Washington Chapter and the Grand Lodge. This means that he didn't become a mason until after his return from India at the end of his term as general-manager of Hume Pipes in India.

Paul went on to add:

> At his [Frank's] funeral there was a section where the local secretary took part of the service using the Masonic Committal. Mother did not like the Masons (I never found out why, other than that Father joined only a year after I was born - possibly losing two children before me had a bearing also). She acceded to their request because Father would have wanted it.

London — June 16, 2001

I go into battle again with the Supreme Court and send the protho-notary a list of questions:

- Who was the presiding judge at the original divorce hearing?
- Who were the solicitors representing the two parties?
- Were there legal representatives of any other persons or organisations at the hearing?
- Who was the judge (or judges) who ruled in the past three years that the divorce papers must not be shown to Mr Paul Paice, myself or anyone else?
- Was there a specific reason given for this ruling?

London — June 29, 2001

At the suggestion of Rosemary Varty, I write to the Victorian State

Attorney-General, Rob Hulls, appealing for his help. It is a very long shot, but I am desperate to explore all possible routes. I summarise my case and conclude with these points:

1. It is now more than 80 years since the divorce was granted.
2. The parties directly involved have been dead more than forty years.
3. The only child of the parties is a joint applicant.
4. The original divorce hearing was held in an open court.
5. The court documents have been retrospectively made confidential for undisclosed reasons.
6. Had the divorce taken place two years earlier, the files would have been open for public scrutiny in the Public Records Office. The closure of the file without adequate explanation runs counter to the spirit of the Freedom of Information Act.

Melbourne — July 4, 2001

The Supreme Court prothonotary's office writes to me in response to my June 16 letter stating that "due to confidentiality" it could not provide the name of Florrie Cox's solicitors for the divorce hearing, though, inexplicably, I was given the name of Frank Paice's solicitors. These were Maddock, Jamieson and Lonie, now reduced to the simple name Maddocks, one of the biggest firms of solicitors in Melbourne and Sydney. The letter also informs me that the presiding judge was Mr Justice Hood — Sir Joseph Henry Hood, who retired from the bench about two years after hearing the case and who died the following year.

I make a note to enquire whether Mr Justice Hood had a connection with Freemasonry.

London — July 11, 2001

I write back to the prothonotary's office, complaining about its refusal to give me the name of Florrie's solicitors and about its failure to answer my question whether any other persons or organisations were legally represented at the hearing. This second issue may not seem important, but I want to know if Olga Johnston or the Baptist Mission Society had a direct legal interest in the case.

My letter of complaint also raises what, to me, is another important issue:

I am astonished that the Prothonotary has refused to give me the name/s of the judge or judges who recently ruled that the Paice divorce file must never be revealed to anyone, ever. I use the word "astonished" advisedly, as this refusal runs counter to democratic and judicial openness in this modern age. What possible excuse can there be for not giving me the name of the judge?

I would be grateful for an early explanation, as I intend to follow this matter through.

London — July 15, 2001

I try another possibility: the Victorian Civil Liberties Council [since renamed Liberty Victoria]. I email the president, Chris Maxwell QC, who replies within hours, promising to look into the matter, but warning that time and resources are "rather limited".

London — July 16, 2001

A fax is received from the Victorian Supreme Court Library, responding to my request for information about Mr Justice Hood. There are two biographies, neither of which indicate that he was a Freemason.

Melbourne — July 27, 2001

The Department of Justice writes back, responding to my letter of June 29 to the Attorney-General, Rob Hulls MP. The Assistant Director of Court Services, John Lynch, makes the following points:

The Supreme Court is vested with the authority to decide if access is granted to a Supreme Court file. No provision for access to these files is made in the Freedom of Information Act 1982.

In order to obtain access to a Supreme Court file an application must be made directly to the Court. I understand from your correspondence, and from my subsequent enquiries at the Supreme Court that you have made several applications to gain access to the file relating to the divorce of your great aunt, Florence Martha Paice, and Frank Ernest Paice.

I am advised that your application was considered by a Judge, who decided that only some of the information from the file would be released to you.

The Supreme Court further advise that they generally do not release personal information documented in court files.

You will appreciate that because the Court operates independently of Government neither the Attorney-General, nor officers of this Department is in a position to take this matter any further.

I have to admit to myself that the points made in this letter about the separation of the court and government are entirely valid in a democratic society.

London — August 6, 2001

A Freemason friend in Melbourne tells me that Mr Justice Hood was apparently not in the Masons. So, it would appear that is one area of suspicion that fades away.

Brisbane — August 12, 2001

Rev. Cyril Baldwin, the former missionary in Bengal, dies at Ipswich in Queensland at the age of 104. His passing at such a grand old age happens as I am preparing to leave London for another visit to Australia. Sadly, I have now missed my opportunity to visit and question the one living person to have had first-hand knowledge of what happened to Frank, Florrie and Olga in Bengal.

Melbourne — August 15, 2001

The prothonotary's office replies to my complaint of July 17 with a firm brush-off:

> Your application was heard by a Judge in the Practice Court and it is not necessary to advise you who made the decision regarding the access to the file. Secondly, the only solicitor details on the file have already been forwarded to you. I cannot advise you of the other parties' solicitor details as this was not contained in the court records.
>
> I do apologise for any inconvenience caused, but as previously advised this is the only information that can be released to you.

This is another setback, but it does suggest that Florrie did not have legal representation in court during the divorce hearing.

It could be argued from my recent exchanges with the Supreme Court that I should stop bashing my head against the proverbial brick wall. But I am not easily discouraged and vow to press on.

Melbourne — August 23, 2001

The Supreme Court prothonotary, Joe Saltalamacchia, agrees to meet me again. We spend more than an hour together discussing how I might get the information I wanted. He is friendly and sympathetic, but unable to help because of the renewed ruling that the file must be closed for all time. He is, however, able to explain that the hearing was a special annulment divorce. This means that in the court's eyes, the marriage was never consummated, rather than having broken down.

Joe sits across the meeting room table from me with the divorce file in front of him. Tantalisingly, it is barely a metre from me. At one point, I resort to the old journalistic device of suggesting that he might need to visit the toilet, giving me the unspoken opportunity to have a quick flick through the file during his absence. He laughs knowingly and is having none of it.

Despairingly, I tell Joe that there seems no alternative for me than to spend money on a barrister to make a formal application to the court. His reply surprises me: "You don't need to do that, you could do it yourself". He tells me to prepare a statutory declaration, stating who I am, why I wanted to see the file, and what the attitude to opening the file would be from other members in Florrie Cox's family and from Frank Paice's son, Paul. If I do that, a hearing can be arranged in the following week.

Immediately after the meeting, I phone Paul Paice to advise him of this and he offers to provide a supporting letter to the court, if I will type it for him. Cathy Fry, a solicitor in the legal firm that employs my cousin Helen Spong, agrees to assist me with the statutory declaration first thing the next morning.

Among the points I make are these two:

> I believe the tragic and gripping story of my great aunt will be an important commentary on the consequences of the social, sexual and religious attitudes that existed in Australia in the first half of the 20th century.

> I sincerely believe that my gaining access to the divorce files will clarify a number of issues concerning the circumstances of my great aunt's marriage. It is now more than 80 years since the events took place, and I do not believe that any embarrassment will be caused to surviving relatives.

In his supporting letter to the court, Paul explains that he cannot attend the hearing himself because he has commitments as a volunteer driver for the Eastern Volunteer Resource Centre in Ringwood, a Melbourne suburb, but says he is happy to have me represent his interests.

He also states:

> Ian Richardson has kept me informed of his research into my father's marriage to his great aunt. My father told me that he had been married before to a Miss Cox who could not have children, but I did not know the details. I am now extremely interested to know the circumstances of his divorce. As I am the only living person who is directly affected, I cannot understand why my earlier requests to the court for information were rejected.

Melbourne — August 30, 2001

I email my family back in London, describing today as "a most fantastic day". That is no exaggeration, for after a battle lasting about 18 months, I have been granted access to the Supreme Court's records on the divorce of Florrie and Frank.

While memories of what happened are fresh in my mind, I make these notes:

> I arrived at the Victorian Supreme Court just before noon, expecting to make my appearance in a courtroom, but was ushered into the chambers of Mr Justice [Barry] Beach. Though it was just him and me and the prothonotary, the hearing was quite formal, requiring some modest bowing and "Your Honours", but I was allowed to sit in one of the judge's comfy leather chairs while he asked me a series of pertinent questions before announcing that he would allow me full access to the file. I asked if this meant I could photocopy the file and he agreed I could. The hearing lasted about 20 minutes.

> The main concern for Mr Justice Beach seemed to be that no-one would be hurt by the revelations in the file. The fact that Paul Paice was a joint applicant appeared to be an important factor. Also, it had become clear that I knew many of the facts anyway.

> Mr Justice Beach was, I would guess, close to 70 years old. He didn't look especially healthy and wore woollen gloves with the ends cut off the fingers. I guess he must be suffering from arthritis. His manner was friendly and to the point. He was curious to know more about Florrie's medical condition, but otherwise stuck strictly to the matter of the file. [He has since retired from the bench.]

My excitement can barely be contained as I am escorted to the court photocopying room by Joe Saltalamacchia. I turn to him with a grin: "You knew this would happen, didn't you!" He shakes his head and replies: "No I didn't," adding the jaw-dropping punchline: "He was the judge who recently confirmed that the file should remain closed for all time."

On being handed the much-desired divorce file, I see that there are about 60 pages. I go to the photocopying machine and run off two copies – one for me and one for Paul.

19 The evidence revealed

Melbourne — August 30, 2001

After delivering a copy of the divorce file to Paul Paice, I sit down at my mother's home in Blackburn to study my copy in detail. It reveals information that is both fascinating and deeply sad.

It also raises some most important questions, not least the exceptional speed with which the divorce/annulment was granted in an age when divorces were fairly rare and normally took several years to process. This reinforces my suspicion that Olga Johnston was pregnant by Frank and that it was felt in the church's greater interests that the matter be settled hastily.

Frank Paice's petition to the Supreme Court to declare his marriage to Florrie null and void was dated April 9, 1919 – less than six months after the scandal broke and Frank was dismissed as a Baptist missionary. The petition states in part:

THAT on the 23rd. day of December 1914 a ceremony of marriage was in fact celebrated between Your Petitioner and Florence Martha Cox the abovenamed Respondent at Calcutta India by the Reverend W. Norledge according to the rites of the Baptist Church.

THAT at the time when the said ceremony of marriage was celebrated the said Respondent was, and ever since has been, and still is unable to consummate the same by reason of the malformation frigidity or other defect of the parts of generation of the said Respondent and such defect is incurable by art or skill and will so appear upon inspection.

An associated affidavit from Frank provides a useful chronology:

I, FRANK ERNEST PAICE of Fuchsia Street Blackburn in the State of Victoria the abovenamed Petitioner make oath and say :-

THAT the statements contained in Paragraphs 1 and 2 of my Petition filed in the above Cause are true.

THAT I am 30 years of age and was born at Christchurch New Zealand and am domiciled in the State of Victoria.

THE said Respondent is 31 years of age or thereabouts and was born in Victoria and is domiciled in the said State of Victoria.

BEFORE marriage I was a Bachelor and a Theological Student and after marriage I followed the occupation of a Missionary and Superintendent of Technical Schools in India.

THE said Respondent before marriage was a Spinster and earned her livelihood as a Shop Assistant and after marriage was maintained and supported by me.

IMMEDIATELY after the said ceremony of marriage Respondent and I went to reside at Mymensingh East Bengal India where we remained for a period of about 4 months when we moved to Faridpur East Bengal aforesaid where we resided until the month of December 1918 when the Respondent returned to Melbourne and went to reside with her parents.

FOR a period of 2 years prior to the Respondent leaving for Melbourne as aforesaid although living in the same Bungalow we lived entirely apart owing to the circumstances mentioned in Paragraph 9 hereof.

I continued to reside in India until the month of January 1919 when I returned to Victoria and since my return to Victoria the Respondent and I have lived separate and apart owing to the causes aforesaid.

THAT from time to time since the said ceremony of marriage was celebrated I attempted to have sexual intercourse with the said Respondent so as to consummate the said marriage but found that I was unable to do so by reason of the malformation frigidity or other defect of the parts of generation of the said Respondent.

THERE are no children issue of the said marriage.

SAVE as aforesaid there have been no separation or separations between me and the said Respondent.

I distinctly and unequivocally deny all collusion or connivance past or present direct or indirect with the Respondent.

There are two points that I particularly note:

1. The time when Frank and Florrie began to lead separate lives in Faridpur coincides with the holiday they took with Olga in Kashmir in October 1916. This reinforces my hunch that this was probably when Frank's friendship with Olga developed into a serious illicit affair.

2. The documents refer to Florrie as "Florence Martha Paice (otherwise known as Florence Martha Cox)". This would suggest that

she had already reverted informally to her maiden name by the time the court case began. Certainly, the electoral roll for the Australian Federal Elections in December 1919 lists her by her maiden name. The addresses at the time of the hearing are listed as Fuchsia Street, Blackburn, for Frank, and Belmore Road, Balwyn, for Florrie.

There now follows a further submission to the court by Frank's legal representatives:

Divorce and Matrimonial Causes Jurisdiction

FRANK ERNEST PAICE Petitioner
- and -
FLORENCE MARTHA PAICE (otherwise FLORENCE MARTHA COX) Respondent

I, HENRY CLARNETTE of 15 Yarra Grove Hawthorn in the State of Victoria Clerk to Maddock Jamieson and Lonie of 136 and 138 Queen Street Melbourne Solicitors for the Petitioner make oath and say as follows:-

1. I did on the twenty-fifth day of April 1919 personally serve the Respondent herein with a true copy of the Summons now produced and shown to me marked with the letter "A" and with a true copy of the Affidavit of the above-named Petitioner sworn the twenty-fourth day of April 1919 and a true copy of the Affidavit of John Henry Maddock sworn the twenty-fifth day of April 1919 by delivering such true copy Summons and Affidavits of the Petitioner and John Henry Maddock to the said Respondent in person at Belmore Road Balwyn.

2. THE time for entering appearance to the Citation herein by the Respondent expired on the twenty-fourth day of April 1919.

3. ON the twenty-fifth day of April 1919 I duly searched in the Office of the Prothonotary of this Court and found that no appearance had been entered by or on behalf of the Respondent.

4. THIS suit has been set down for hearing before a Judge without a Jury at the May sittings of this court.

So, at this stage it seems from the court records that Florrie is not seeking to challenge the annulment petition.

Here is the exchange of letters between Frank's solicitor, J. H. Maddock, and Florrie:

Mrs. F. M. Paice,
c/o Mrs. A. P. Cox [Florrie's mother],
Belmore Road,
Deepdene.

Dear Madam,

We have been instructed by your husband to take proceedings to obtain the nullification of your marriage on the ground that the marriage has not been consummated owing to physical malformation or inability on your part and as it will be necessary to apply to the Court for an Order that you should be medically examined we shall be glad if you would inform us of the name of your Solicitor or if you have no Solicitor acting for you if you would see our Mr. Maddock as soon as possible as it is necessary for Mr. Paice to leave the Colony for India at an early date.

Yours truly, MADDOCK JAMIESON & LONIE

IN reply to such letter I received a letter from the Respondent of which the following is a copy:-

Belmore Road,
Deepdene,
6/4/19.

Maddock Jamieson & Lonie, Solicitors

Dear Sirs,

I am in receipt of your letter dated second April 1919 and as I have no Solicitor wish to make an appointment to meet Mr. Maddock at his Office on Tuesday morning at 11 o'clock.

Yours truly,
F. M. PAICE

ON the eighth instant at 11 o'clock the Respondent saw me accompanied by her brother [not stated which one]. I read to them the Petition in this matter and explained to them the nature of the Petitioner's complaint as stated in his Affidavit sworn and filed herein. I further told them that in view of the allegations made by the petitioner an Order would probably be made by the Court that the Respondent should submit herself to medical examination for the purpose of verifying or otherwise the allegations made by the Petitioner.

THE Respondent in reply said that the allegations were correct and that she would not submit herself to examination. I then told her that the result of such a course might be that the Court would decree that the marriage between herself and the Petitioner was null and void without her being heard but that she could at any time before the Decree was pronounced change her mind and appear and give evidence before the Court. She replied that she thought under the circumstances that it was better to let the case go on. Her brother who was present then asked whether the Petitioner was going to make any allowance. I replied that no arrangement of any kind could be made at all and asked whether it would not be as well that Respondent should see a Solicitor on the matter and to this Respondent simply replied "No". They then withdrew.

We can only guess at just how painful these exchanges must have been for Florrie and it is understandable that she would not want to heap humiliation upon humiliation by undergoing an intrusive medical examination.

I note that again Florrie is accompanied by one of her brothers. This is not necessarily significant, but I can't help wondering why her parents seem to play no public, or even semi-public, part in supporting her through a hugely difficult time. Is this further evidence that Florrie's mother, in particular, was too embarrassed or unsympathetic to offer the level of backing that a mother should have given a daughter in distress?

On April 24, 1919 Frank Paice submits a further, rather surprising declaration to the Supreme Court:

> I have made arrangement with Messieurs Bird and Company General Merchants of the Chartered Bank Buildings Calcutta India to go to India to take up a position with it and I have booked my passage by the Steamship *SS Houtaman* [should read *SS Houtman*] which was to have left Victoria for India about the middle of April 1919, but the time of the said Steamship's departure has been definitely fixed for the third day of May 1919. It is imperative for me to return to India otherwise I will lose an important engagement and the state of my finances are such that I cannot afford to do so.

> I am desirous that an Order be made that I be examined on oath *de bene esse* before a judge of the Supreme Court or any Officer thereof or any other person appointed by a Judge of the Supreme Court prior to my departure for India.

The declaration is surprising because it reveals that Frank originally planned to take up a post with Bird and Company and not as I had believed with the Australian-owned company, Hume Pipes of India.

I have found no information about why the Bird and Company appointment apparently came to nothing, or was so short-lived, but in Frank's haste to get to India, he also sought the court's agreement to give his evidence — *de bene esse**, to use the Latin legal term — in advance of the annulment hearing that would deliver judgement.

*to act provisionally or in anticipation of a future occasion; to take evidence for future use while it is available.

> BY CONSENT IT IS ORDERED that two duly qualified medical Practitioners one to be nominated by or on behalf of the Petitioner and one to be nominated by or on behalf of the Respondent be appointed Medical Inspectors to examine and inspect and report in writing upon the part and organs of generation of Frank Ernest Paice the Petitioner in this Cause and of Florence Martha Paice (otherwise Florence Martha Cox) the Respondent in this Cause whether he or she is capable

of performing the act of generation and if incapable of so doing whether such impotency can or cannot be relieved or removed by art or skill and whether he or she hath or hath not any impediment on his or her part to prevent the consummation of Marriage.

Mr Justice Hood then orders the medical inspectors to present their reports to the-then prothonotary, Mr Denis F. McGrath.

The document also answers one of my key questions about whether the main hearing was held behind closed doors. It shows that Mr Justice Hood crossed out such a request. This confirms that the hearing was held in open court, technically at least:

> . . .AND IT IS FURTHER ORDERED that the abovenamed Petitioner be examined *viva voce** in Melbourne before Joseph Arthur Richardson Esquire Associate to His Honor Mr. Justice Hood on the first day of May 1919 at 11.0 o'clock in the forenoon AND IT IS FURTHER ORDERED that the examination so taken be filed in the Prothonotary's Office of the Supreme Court and that an office copy or copies thereof may be read and given in evidence on the trial of this Cause.

> DATED the 28th day of April 1919.
> Signed by Mr Justice Hood [Sir Joseph Henry Hood]

> *Legalese for "living voice" — an oral, as against written, examination.

We now move forward to May 6, 1919 when the chosen medical inspector, Dr John Reginald Davis of May Street, Port Melbourne, submits his report to the Supreme Court:

> I have faithfully and to the best of my skill inspected and examined the parts and organs of generation of the abovenamed Frank Ernest Paice the Petitioner in this cause and report on such inspection and examination that (a) the said Frank Paice the abovementioned Petitioner is capable of performing the act of generation (b) the said Frank Paice hath not any impediment on his part to prevent the consummation of marriage.

We are left to speculate on the detail of this examination. For example, did he require Frank to prove that he could get an erection? Whatever, it must have been a further acute embarrassment for him.

Dr Davis's report then continues:

> I DO FURTHER REPORT that I have not inspected or examined the parts and organs of generation of Florence Martha Paice. The said Respondent did not submit herself to my inspection and examination.

On May 1, 1919 Frank submitted himself for an oral examination by the judge's associate, Mr J. A. Richardson. Frank was accompanied by his legal counsel, Mr Woolf.

There was no appearance by Florrie or a legal representative.

In a hand-written record of the examination, Frank states that he will leave for India on the *SS Houtman* on May 3 and will be away for many months.

He then gives his account of what happened on the honeymoon:

> On the first night of the marriage, I made no attempt to have intercourse with the Respondent. Within a night or two later I made my first attempt to have it. I had a proper erection and was quite capable of having intercourse. I could not get my penis into the vagina beyond an inch [2.5 centimetres]. My penis met with an obstruction. The Respondent complained that it hurt her.

Nothing more is recorded about what must have been a very, very fraught honeymoon, but Frank goes on to explain what later happened:

> From time to time during the next two years I tried to have intercourse with the Respondent. I was never able to do so on account of meeting with this obstruction in the vagina. On each occasion I had a proper erection and was quite capable.

> For the first month I could not get my penis into her vagina for more than about an inch; my penis came into contact with the obstruction in the Respondent's vagina every time. Later, I got my penis in a little more than an inch by pushing hard against the obstruction.

Frank declares that this state of affairs continued for the first two years of the marriage and that during that time he had never been able to achieve full penetration. He goes on to recount what must have been traumatic times for both Frank and Florrie:

> On several occasions I asked the Respondent to try to assist me by putting my penis in the right place. She tried to direct it. She said that it slipped away from the place she wished it to go. She said she could not put it into the right place. She later gave up attempting to assist me. She complained frequently that I hurt her.

While Frank appears to have shown some sympathy for Florrie's situation, he is obviously angry about one aspect:

> On many occasions I told her I was unable to have proper connection with her and asked her to go to see a doctor to be examined to see what was the matter with her. She refused to do so. She gave no reason for her refusal.

Finally, Frank's attempts to consummate the marriage end:

> I said to the Respondent after this first two years: "It is no use going on like this, as I cannot have proper connection". I ceased my attempts to have intercourse. The Respondent never complained in any way at my ceasing my attempts to have connection with her.

So, we now know the prime reason why the marriage failed: an inability to consummate it because of an obstruction in the vagina. But how did that "obstruction" come about? Was it simply a peculiar vaginal malformation — perhaps unique to Florrie — or was there some other cause? These questions will have to be explored further at an early opportunity.

As I continue to study the court file, I see an affidavit dated May 20, 1919 from Frank's solicitor, J. H. Maddock, stating that Frank left Australia, as planned, on May 3 on the *SS Houtman*. I cannot find a record of that ship's particular voyage, so am unable to establish if Olga Johnston travelled back to India with him or followed later. This is of no special importance, but it would have been interesting nonetheless.

There then followed hearings at the Supreme Court on May 20 and 29, but there is no record of what took place at these, though there is a reference to "several witnesses". However, on June 5, Mr Justice Hood hands down his judgement in the absence of Frank and, probably, Florrie, although Frank's counsel Mr Woolf was present.

Here are extracts from the tortuous declaration written by the Supreme Court's chief clerk, Mr N. Phillips:

> UPON HEARING the said Petition and the evidence of the several witnesses called on behalf of the Petitioner taken upon their oral examination at the hearing and what was alleged by Mr. Woolf of Counsel for the Petitioner AND UPON READING the evidence of the Petitioner taken *de bene esse* . . . and the Report of the Medical Inspector nominated by or on behalf of the Petitioner appointed to examine the Petitioner and Respondent and the several Exhibits therein and the Affidavit of John Henry Maddock . . . as to the absence of the Petitioner from the State of Victoria and filed herein THIS COURT DOTH ORDER AND DECREE that the marriage . . . be pronounced and declared to have been and to be absolutely null and void to all intents and purposes in the law whatsoever by reason of the malformation frigidity or other defect of the parts of generation of the said Respondent and such defect is incurable by art or skill and that the said Petitioner be pronounced to have been and to be free from all bond of marriage with the said Respondent unless within 3 months from the date of this Decree Nisi sufficient cause be shewn to this Court why this Decree Nisi should not be made absolute.

The reference to "several witnesses" called on behalf of Frank is interesting. Who were they? And what did they have to say? We will most likely never know.

The file includes a warning to both Frank and Florrie that if either marries before the decree nisi is made absolute they will be guilty of bigamy.

On September 6, 1919, the prothonotary, Mr McGrath, issues a declaration that the decree nisi has been made absolute. In signing the declaration he has corrected "dissolution of marriage" to "nullity of marriage":

I, DENIS FRANCIS McGRATH Prothonotary of the Supreme court of the State of Victoria HEREBY CERTIFY that the Decree Nisi for nullity of Marriage herein granted the fifth day of June One thousand nine hundred and nineteen has been made absolute.

GIVEN under my hand and the Seal of the Supreme Court of the State of Victoria at Melbourne this sixth day of September One thousand nine hundred and nineteen.

D. F. McGrath
Prothonotary

And that was it. An abrupt end to a very troubled, tragic marriage.

20 More questions

London — early September, 2001

As recounted in Chapter 5, Frank and Olga were married in a civil ceremony in Calcutta on October 14, 1919 – just over five weeks after the annulment was made absolute.

Florrie remained in Australia, mostly working for the Cox family in its suburban newsagency and stationery business. She was, however, living in Geelong for a time with her sister, Amelia "Minnie" Brew, and husband John, between her return to Australia and the divorce. I learn this from the birth certificate of Minnie and John's son, Edward. Florrie was the "informant" and signed the certificate as "F. M. Paice". She gave her address as 270 McKillop Street, East Geelong, where the Brew family lived.

Presumably, as well as helping out her sister with the birth, Florrie's absence from Melbourne in the run-up to the divorce judgement minimised family embarrassment. However, the electoral rolls show that Florrie was back in Melbourne and had reverted to her maiden name in time for the December 1919 Australian Federal Elections. By then, of course, Frank and Olga had returned to India and were married and Florrie was making determined efforts to establish a new life for herself.

Access to the Supreme Court file has given me vital information that could lead me to identifying Florrie's medical condition, but it still doesn't explain why such a juicy case failed to make it into the newspapers. The Melbourne *Truth* would normally have given over a page or two to such a court hearing, involving as it did that staple of tabloid journalism, sex, scandal and religion. So, why didn't it? Even if neither Frank nor Florrie attended the hearings, the newspaper court reporters would surely have been alerted to the case and gained access to the evidence as it was tabled in open court. My suspicion is that a decision was made jointly by the *Truth* and Melbourne's other newspapers, *The Argus*, *The Age* and *The Herald* not to run anything, but I need to investigate how this might have come about.

Another question: Would it have been an option for Florrie to have counter-petitioned for divorce on the grounds of Frank's presumed adultery with Olga? Possibly, but that would probably have made the situation even messier with no end benefit for Florrie.

I decide to see what Google and the Internet might reveal about Florrie's vaginal blockage. It doesn't take long to track down the strong possibility that Florrie was born with a rare condition called CAIS, the complete form of a condition called Androgen Insensitivity Syndrome (AIS). This is a eureka moment, but in view of the false trails I have been led down before, I need to make further investigations before coming to a firm conclusion.

If it were CAIS, then Florrie would have been born with male XY chromosomes, but due to hormonal dysfunction while in the womb, she would have had the appearance of a woman, but without any internal female organs and with very little or no under-arm or pubic hair. As she would have had no reproductive organs, she could not have menstruated. This raises important questions about how much Florrie or her mother and sisters knew of her condition.

My enquiries confirm that the secrecy surrounding sexual matters in upright religious families was such that it would be quite usual for a young girl never to know that she would acquire pubic hair or have periods as she approached adulthood. Nudity, even among females in the same family, was strictly taboo.

In the rare event of Florrie stumbling across paintings or statues of nudes, this would not have alerted her that something was amiss as the genitalia in works of art was usually covered by strategically-placed clothing or presented as hairless. Not that Florrie or her family would have felt it was right to take an interest in such "improper" art.

While researching *God's Triangle* I spoke to several elderly women relatives about what it was like for them on reaching puberty. Their experiences came two or three decades after Florrie was a young woman, but they told me that nothing much had changed. There was absolutely no nudity in the family. Women got dressed in private, though men were less bothered about being seen naked by other men.

In all cases, these women relatives were shocked and very frightened when they experienced their first menstrual bleeding, as they had not been forewarned. One told me that she thought she was going to die. As it was before sanitary towels became widely available in shops, it was the first she knew of the purpose of all the secretly-washed bits of rag that would regularly appear on the clothes line.

It seems incredible that in an age when it was the norm to have big families, older sisters would not feel able to alert their younger siblings to the imminence of menstruation. And even when menstruation began, a sensible, informed explanation was rarely offered. Instead, it was mostly dismissed as just some sort of burden women had to bear with Christian fortitude and not be talked about. In many religious communities — not just Christian ones — little has changed, even today.

London — September 16 and 17, 2001

I exchange emails with researcher Ros Gooden about the report that Frank Paice's clergyman brother, Rev. George W. Paice, had moved himself and his family to South Australia to escape the scandal resulting from Frank's dismissal from the missionary service.

It is not possible to establish precise dates, but while Frank was stationed in Bengal, George remained in Victoria and spent spells in charge of the Baptist churches in Traralgon, Wandin North and Lilydale, then finally, Barton Street, Hawthorn in Melbourne. Late in 1918 — probably in October, the month after the scandal broke — the family moved interstate, where George accepted a posting as minister at a cluster of three Baptist churches on the Yorke Peninsula.

Apart from other considerations, it is unlikely that the family scandal would have filtered through to such remote locations. After several other rural postings, George moved to Adelaide where he remained.

Melbourne — December 21, 2001

Paul Paice emails me to give some more information about his grandfather, William George "Willie" Paice, who was a lay preacher. He had grown up at One Tree Hill in the Dandenong Mountains, just outside Melbourne. He was a market gardener there and would take his fruit and vegetables to market by horse and cart.

Melbourne — April 13, 2002

Paul emails me with still more information about his grandfather.

He tells me that after retiring, Willie lived with Frank and Olga for a while, but this didn't work out. According to Paul, "Mother must have had some difference [with Willie] and he had moved to a friend's in Box Hill, quite close by". Paul thought these friends were related to Frank Sedgman, the Australian tennis champion.

Paul did not know what the problem was between his mother and Willie, but it was further evidence that Olga seemed to have difficulty getting along with many people.

London — May 30, 2002

Paul and Lin Paice are visiting Britain and Paul reviews the results of my research.

As I am going to be in Melbourne again before Paul and Lin have returned home from their travels, he arranges for me to contact his daughter, Suzanne Christian, to inspect the Paice family bible.

Melbourne — June 13, 2002

I meet Suzanne by arrangement at Paul and Lin's house in Blackburn. We find the family bible. It contains quite a bit of information about births, deaths and marriages, but nothing that is particularly relevant to Frank and Olga's time in India.

I mention my plans for *God's Triangle*, but she asks no questions.

London — July 18, 2002

On my return home, I had been talking to a psychiatrist who lives near us. Our conversation turned to the *God's Triangle* project and she expressed an interest in seeing Florrie's medical reports from Mont Park. I tell her about my suspicions that Florrie was born with Complete Androgen Insensitivity Syndrome. She had not heard of this condition, but agreed to study the Mont Park file.

She emails me today with some thoughts on the reports:

> I am not sure that one could diagnose with confidence her as suffering from schizophrenia based only on what's in the notes. It could have also been psychotic depression, as you thought yourself.

> There probably were delusions but they could be attributed to the depression. I don't know how she was treated and obviously at that point not many drugs were available. I believe that if one had that problem today they would not have to spend their life in hospital. but would probably need brief admissions.

> The other thing that crossed my mind is whether Complete Androgen Insensitivity Syndrome is related to psychiatric symptoms. You see quite often when you have

endocrine abnormalities there can be some psychopathology. We don't know though what her hormones were like and I don't know if there is any research supporting this hypothesis.

Anyhow, I thought it was a rather sad but interesting story.

21 Investigating Calcutta

Calcutta — November 22-29, 2002

My younger son, Niall, and I fly to Kolkata, but best known as Calcutta, to do further research on Florrie, Frank and Olga and to get a sense of what life would have been like when they were there.

Here are extracts from the report I did at the time:

The Baptist Mission Society Guest House, which is where Florrie Cox, Hedley Sutton, Frank Paice and Olga Johnston would have usually stayed during their visits to Calcutta, is a large cement-rendered brick building, set in spacious gardens. It is in what used to be called Circular Road, but which has since been re-named A. J. C. Bose Road. Next door is the Circular Road Baptist Church where Florrie Cox and Frank Paice were married in December 1914, and a few doors away, in the opposite direction, is the *Mother House*, set up by the late Mother Theresa.

The Fredericks, who now run the guest house, were just arising as we arrived [from the airport], so Niall and I had a cup of tea and a wander around the grounds. There were a couple of pet white rabbits hopping about and dozens of squawking crows on the lawns and in the trees. Birds of prey — identified by Niall as being from the kite family — circled lazily overhead. As we were to discover, there were almost as many crows as people in Kolkata, and the sky during the daylight hours always had an abundance of circling kites.

The Fredericks, a charming Anglo-Indian retired business couple, came downstairs about 9am. We were warmly welcomed and invited to sit in on morning devotions for the staff. I was completely thrown when Patsy Frederick sprung it on me that I should lead the opening prayer. I declined, stammering something about jetlag. She happily took this at face value and led the prayer herself.

The devotions, which lasted for about 20 minutes, were very upbeat with several action songs and an amusing (deliberately amusing, I think) sermon delivered by a 70-year-old Indian woman from across town somewhere. The theme for her sermon was the drink "7 Up". I can't remember all seven "ups", but they included "get up", "cheer up", "speak up" (for Jesus) and "shut up" (when you have only unpleasant things to say). The dozen male and female staff – all Indian – were neatly turned out in brown uniforms bearing the BMS logo. They threw themselves enthusiastically into the devotions, which was rather surprising when I was later to learn that two-thirds of them were either Hindus or Muslims. Presumably, a daily dose of the Christian message is a requirement of their employment.

Stephen Frederick, who used to be in the tea business, rounded up a van and driver and took us through the peak hour traffic to our accommodation.

The water is highly dangerous for Europeans and others not brought up with it. The fact is that the sewers and the mains water supplies in Kolkata have an uncomfortably-close co-existence. We were frequently warned that under no circumstances should we touch water from household or street taps – at least not unless it was well and truly boiled. To do otherwise would most likely result in our spending the rest of the visit on the toilet or in hospital.

Malaria is endemic in Kolkata. Niall and I have had to take a five-week course of anti-malarial tablets, and whenever we stepped outside our guest house, we had to remember to first spray our bare skin with "jungle strength" insect repellent. It is a sobering thought that the connection between mosquitoes and malaria was not confirmed until 1898 – just five years before Hedley Sutton arrived in Bengal to begin work as a missionary. And then there were the ever-present threats of TB, cholera, smallpox and typhoid, just to name four nasty diseases.

Many buildings — even grand houses — did not have glass or screens in their windows because the weather was so hot and humid all year round. Internal doors were usually left open to allow the air to circulate. When privacy was required, a curtain would be drawn across the doorway. Mosquito nets would be used at night, but only if the mosquitoes became too irritating.

Kolkata is a relatively young city for such an old country, in that it was built by the country's British rulers about three hundred years ago and was until 1911 India's capital. I would love to have seen the city in its heyday. The elegant buildings, built along wide avenues and around vast parks, were stunning and must have made it one of the great cities of the world. Today, most of the original buildings are derelict, with the inhabitants of Kolkata showing little or no interest in them being restored.

There was an embarrassing moment when I made a return visit to the BMS to give Patsy Frederick a file of all the historical stuff Rosemary and I had gathered about the various Bengal mission stations early in the 1900s. It was the Saturday afternoon and she wished to know where I would be worshipping the next day. I had to tell her that I wouldn't be worshipping anywhere and that I was not a believer. This provoked a full-on evangelical offensive, with Patsy telling me that I couldn't possibly be a truly happy person without taking Jesus into my heart.

Our rather extended debate ended in a friendly draw. I expressed understanding of her religious position, while she agreed (reluctantly, I think) that it was possible to be a moral, happy person without being a Christian.

Niall and I witnessed a daily sermon that would be regarded in most Western countries as outrageously politically incorrect. It was illustrated by a variety of items of different colours. The black item represented sin and our hearts before becoming a Christian. The red item represented "the blood of Christ" which would wash away the sin. The white was after Jesus had made our hearts "as white as snow", while the gold item represented "the paths of gold" in heaven. Quite fundamentalist stuff. I daresay that if a religious figure in Britain or Australia delivered a sermon equating black with sin, they would probably attract some very nasty publicity and possibly get the sack.

I came across an accommodation block for the staff. I was shocked to find that the servants lived in small and rather squalid single rooms. One man showed me the accommodation for himself, his wife and their two children. It was a room about four metres square with a concrete floor, some basic cooking facilities and a bed. The walls were covered with patches of black mould. I felt very uncomfortable that the missionaries and their visitors lived in comfortable and very spacious rooms in the main house, while the staff were accommodated in buildings more suitable for animals than human beings.

Which takes me on to the realisation that while the missionaries had a tough time in India — mostly because of the heat and disease — they did often live in rather grand accommodation, in keeping with the accepted view that Europeans could not be expected to live like the locals. They also had servants to do all their cooking, washing, cleaning and gardening.

I managed to locate the large house (6 Rawdon Street, now renamed 6 Sarujini Naidu Sarina) where Florrie Cox lived for a few weeks before getting married to Frank Paice. It is also where their wedding reception was held. It is a few streets from the Circular Road Baptist Church. At the time of the marriage, it was occupied by Mr and Mrs A. P. Stockwell. Mr Stockwell gave Florrie away in the absence of her father.

The house is now rather shabby and owned by a very sophisticated high-born Muslim, Mr Monem, the grandson of a nawab (a kind of duke) in northern Bengal. A retired tea trader, he had three Rolls Royce cars in his garages, and clearly wasn't short of a rupee or two. Mr Monem told me that since the Stockwells occupied the house, two more floors had been added. But the house had been let go in recent years as he planned to demolish it and replace it with a modern block with shops on the ground floor and flats for himself and his family in the floors above.

Mr Monem was an interesting man. In the course of a discussion about the role of missionaries in pre-independence India, he surprised me by coming out strongly in their favour. He told me he had been educated in a Christian school and promptly launched into a recital of the Lord's Prayer. He had also been taught Latin at the school. He said that even in what he called "the wilder parts" of India it was still possible to stumble across a house, all neat and tidy and with a garden and occupied by missionaries, some of whom had spent most of their adult lives working among the locals. He was grateful to the missionaries. "They taught us discipline and a sense of civic duty," he said.

There was no suggestion that Mr Monem was going to abandon his Muslim faith for Christianity. Like most Indians educated in Christian schools, he gratefully accepted the education and happily went along with learning about Christianity, but declined the opportunity to switch faiths. This must have been immensely frustrating for Hedley Sutton and other missionaries who spent so much time educating locals, only to have them walk away at the end of it to resume their lives as Hindus and Muslims. But then my view on this topic is well known: I believe it was perfectly proper to go to India to provide help and education, but wrong to go with the intention of converting the nation to Christianity.

Hedley's mission singularly failed, with only a tiny proportion of the population being Christian after three hundred years of evangelism. But Hedley would be pleased about one thing. It had always been his desire to see local Christians take control of the mission stations in Bengal. And this is the case in many, if not most, instances.

Mr Monem's views on the missionaries run counter to the received wisdom, which is that they were generally regarded with hostility by the British Raj and the majority of locals, particularly the local religious leaders. Indeed, while I was in Kolkata I read a book by a former BBC reporter who made several references to how much missionaries were regarded as "interfering busybodies".

The Circular Road Baptist Church is an impressive building, and unusually for Kolkata, kept in good condition. (See page 19) When Niall and I first visited it, preparations were under way for the Harvest Festival. We didn't stay long, as the minister was not there. We agreed to come back the next day.

When I returned, I was able to meet Pastor Subrata Fullonton and his wife. They live in the spacious house behind the church. I showed him my file, including the photos of Frank Paice, Florrie Cox and Olga Johnston. "Oh," he said, "Olga Johnston. I'm sure there is something about her in our files." Sadly, the room where the files were kept was locked and the treasurer, who had the key, was away until the Monday after we were leaving. We agreed to get in touch again by email after the treasurer had returned. So, I will have to wait to see whether these references throw any light on anything. [I am still waiting, despite a follow-up request.]

Pastor Fullonton was very interested in the wedding photo of Florrie and Frank and we spent some time working out exactly where it had been taken. The conclusion was that it was taken on the lawns at the back of the compound and beside his house. He said the building in the background was not the church, but the bible printing next door. This has since been torn down and replaced with a rather ghastly multi-storey structure, now itself in ruins.

Niall and I spent some time inside the church, which had an austere but cheerful décor. We were amused by a memorial plaque bearing the words "Arrested by the hand of death, 1st February 1839".

I had hoped to track down the Register Office where Frank Paice and Olga Johnston were married in 1919, but had no luck. The marriage record did not specify the location of the office.

I stumbled across a woman marriage registrar in a building just two doors away from our guest house. The woman registrar was very willing to help, but didn't really know where I might find the office.

Darkness fell as we walked back to the guest house, and we came across groups of Muslim men squatting on rugs around pots of food as they ended their daily Ramadan fast.

Further on, we crossed an intersection in one of the main shopping streets where a near-naked man was lying in the foetal position in the gutter. Everyone was just stepping over him. He appeared to be alive, but only just. "Is he okay?" I enquired, asking our guide for the day a very stupid question. "He is okay, sir," he replied, "he is probably just mad. If you try to help him, he will just shout at you. He is comfortable there, sir, and will probably move soon". And so we continued on our way down the street.

It is easy to go along with the view held by many that life is cheap in India. I don't think that is so. They feel the same pain and loss as the rest of us, but do so with greater resignation.

The caste system is unfortunately still alive and well in India, but there is also a tremendous sense of hopelessness when it comes to dealing with so many poor people in such an impoverished country. The social service structure is almost non-existent and there aren't great fleets of police cars and ambulances to come to the aid of every person sick or dying in the streets.

As Niall and I were about to leave Calcutta, I made a donation to the mission society as a "thank you" for the assistance I received. I was told that the money would be used for food and drinks for a Saturday club for poor children in the neighbourhood, but I was disappointed to learn that those invited to the club were expected to spend part of the time "being exposed to the word of our Lord".

Why not provide some entertainment and sustenance for the unfortunate kids and leave it at that? To force them to listen to a Christian sermon seemed to me to be pointless, even counter-productive, and certainly not how I intended my money to be used.

22 A shock for a friend

When carrying out research, luck is almost as important as determined detective work. One such stroke of luck came about in February 2003 when my wife, Rosemary, was in Melbourne and discussing the *God's Triangle* research with longtime friends Sue and Tim James.

A passing reference was made to Frank Paice having been employed by Hume Pipes & Engineering. At this point, Sue and Tim reveal that they knew David Hume, son of the company's founder, the late Walter Hume. They check with David and he agrees to talk to me.

London — March 5, 2003

Rosemary has returned home with David Hume's phone number and I give him a call. I strike pure gold. He is happy to talk and tells me that he had known Frank and Olga on and off for 40 years and had often visited them at their home in Melbourne.

Frank, he says, was "a very nice man", but he was less impressed by Olga. Then comes a surprise. When I ask David what Frank or Olga had told him about their time as missionaries in India, he insists that I must be talking about the wrong people. "Frank was never a missionary; he was an engineer," he declares.

I explain to David that I had irrefutable proof that both Frank and Olga had been missionaries for several years and he is astonished: "Frank was a very nice man, but I had no clue that he had ever been an ordained clergyman and a missionary, though he would never swear or anything like that. As far I knew, he had always been an engineer. Olga was a much tougher person." David also had no idea that it was Frank's second marriage.

David gives me his email address and I promise to send him photographs of Frank, Florrie and Olga.

He says Frank was close to his [David's] parents, who established Hume Pipes & Engineering in Australia and India. Frank did all the design and drawings for a prefabricated steel and concrete house built for the Hume family at Anglesea, a seaside resort in Victoria. David believes it was the first house of its kind in the world. It is still owned by the family.

As far as David knows, his family never realised that Frank had been an ordained minister, but he promises to explore his memory for anecdotes and impressions that might be useful to me.

I suspect that David is wrong in thinking that no-one in his family would have known about Frank's missionary past, although I have no doubt that it was regarded as a taboo subject for discussion and, therefore, would not have been generally known.

I make a note to explore the likelihood that Walter Hume would not have employed a man to run his Indian division without being aware of what Frank had been doing for the first seven or eight years of his adult life. In particular, he must have been briefed about Frank's acknowledged success in managing and expanding the industrial school in Faridpur. Frank's fluency with the Bengali language would have been an enormous asset to Hume's and this, surely, would have been discussed and explained at the top level of the company.

Melbourne — March 9, 2003

David Hume emails me expressing his delight about hearing from me and learning about "the part of Frank that I would never have known about".

He has also viewed the photographs I emailed him. "There is no mistaking Frank," he says, "and Olga comes back to mind from the photo."

David, a man with a mischievous sense of humour, is amused to see Frank and Florrie's wedding photo (see Page 19) with Frank sitting and wearing a clerical collar, while Florrie stands dutifully beside him in her long wedding dress. He observes:

> The original wedding was something, with Frank with his collar back to front. One is tempted to remember the old explanation by father to son as to why he was sitting and mum was standing. "To be truthful son, the picture was taken the day after we were married — I was too tired to stand up, and your mum was too sore to sit down." Not in Frank's case, it seems.

Melbourne — June 3, 2003

Now back in Australia, my researcher Ros Gooden accompanies me on a visit she has arranged for me to meet Olive Paice, the widow of the Rev. Jim Paice, a distant cousin of Frank.

Olive is a resident of the Strathalan Baptist Retirement Village in Melbourne. She is in her mid-eighties and still leading a sprightly life.

She is keen to talk to me, but she knows nothing about Frank and Olga Paice, other than rumours that there had been some sort of matter that had caused a rift between Frank and the rest of the Paices. She says her husband was a keen genealogist and had made many attempts to establish the cause. He had even gone to Adelaide three times to talk to the family of Frank's brother, the Rev. George Paice, but the family had always refused to discuss the matter. She remembers her husband being in tears with frustration at being unable to establish the truth.

She very much wants to know what had happened and I give her a summary. I agree to give her copies of some of the photos and documents in my files.

Olive thinks that George had never been very successful in the ministry in South Australia and she feels this might have been something to do with his being tainted by the family scandal. She also tells me that a "tall thin woman" had once approached her husband Jim at a church assembly and she now thinks this might have been Florrie Cox.

As our meeting draws to a close, Olive is emotional and tells me: "You cannot know how important this day has been to me. If only Jim had been here to hear your story."

Melbourne — June 24, 2003

Ros Gooden passes on an item from *The Australian Baptist* of April 24, 1954, reporting George's death:

> Another who passed to his reward this week was Rev. G. W. Paice, well-known to an earlier generation of Baptists. After a ministry in Victoria, Mr Paice served at Yorketown, Kapunda circuit, Gumeracha and Glen Osmond.
>
> His widow is Sister Paice of the well-known Monreith Hospital. He was a brother of great earnestness and held in high regard by a wide circle of friends. To his widow and two sons, one of whom is married to the daughter of Rev. and Mrs Andrew Gowans, we offer sincere sympathy.

Not surprisingly, the item makes no mention of brother Frank, who by that time had reinvented himself as a pillar of society in Melbourne.

London — June 26, 2003

After my return home, I phone Olive to check that she has received the information I posted to her in Melbourne. She is "very grateful" to have been able to read about Frank and Olga.

Having had time to think about what she had learned from me, she recalls the fact that George Paice's wife, Sister Rosa Henrietta "Nettie" Paice, was the owner of Monreith Private Hospital in Portrush Road, Toorak Gardens, Adelaide. [Monreith is now a nursing home.]

George had worked for Nettie as a kind of odd job man in the hospital after becoming inactive in the church. She thought their son, Clarence "Clarrie", also worked in the hospital. Olive says it must have been what she termed "a proper hospital" because her husband Jim, who was interested in surgery, had once been invited to witness an operation there.

I am keen to know more about the tall woman who approached Jim Paice at the church assembly. Olive says it happened during a Baptist Assembly at the Albert Street Church Hall in Melbourne [now no longer a Baptist building]. She says "a very tall, dignified lady with a very sad face" had handed Jim a scripture book: "You will probably like to have this," the woman said. "It was owned by someone very special to me."

According to Olive, the woman mentioned Frank Paice's name and added "you will probably know this person. I have known and loved him. I would like you to have the book." Olive said the woman then disappeared into the crowd.

When Jim realised what he had been handed, he went looking for the woman, but couldn't find her. The woman was almost certainly Florrie Cox. Olive and I worked it out that the event probably took place around the time Florrie was first admitted to Mont Park in 1945.

Olive recalls that Jim had later given the book to Nettie Paice in the hope that she might respond by revealing the story of Frank to him, but without any luck. Olive can't remember if the book had an inscription.

I ask Olive why it mattered so much to Jim to establish a relation-ship with Frank and George's family. She replies that Jim's parents hadn't wanted him to be a clergyman and he had once sought out the other Paices because they were also ministers. He had hoped there would be "some linkage" with them, but Nettie would never discuss her own family. Although Jim knew that Frank had been a clergyman, he didn't know the circumstances.

Melbourne — August 24, 2003

David Hume emails me in London with an apology for the gap in our communications, but with further useful, considered memories of Frank Paice:

> You have been on my conscience for months, so I shall try to make some sense out of the Family Paice.

> As stated earlier, I had no idea about his history with the Baptist Mission, nor of his first wife. It is a fascinating story.

> As I was born in Oct 1923, it is likely that my memory of the family would be pretty hazy until the 30's.

> My mother used to take me to the Paice house in Nunawading sometimes and I recall that Paul was about my age. He was a much quieter chap than I was, and I do not think we were real friends, but I recall he sometimes came to Kew to spend time with me, and the local lads nearby. I lost touch with him, and have no memory of the last time I saw him.

> Olga seemed to be a stern type of lady to my boy mind, and therefore I do not have too many memories of her.

> I recall Frank from a fairly early age, for he used to come to our house fairly regularly. I am not sure what his job was in the pipe company in those days, but I believe he was involved with the design drawings of the Anglesea house, which replaced the one burnt down in 1929 — so we are talking 1930.

> This house was unique, as it was a prefabricated steel frame, and very light concrete panels bolted in. The main section was octagonal, two stories high - about 30 feet across. Branching out from four of the octagonal sides were three bedrooms, and a kitchen, all single storeys. This is certainly the only house of this structure in Australia, if not the world. I presently occupy the octagonal section and three of the bedrooms.

> My father bought a house on a big hill at Pakenham [Victoria] circa 1931. Frank helped my mother with the renovations.

> In 1938, my father bought a large Victorian house at 24 Howard Street Kew — opposite our home in Studley Park Road. In 1939, it was decided to convert this house into four flats for my four brothers. My mum was in charge of this project, and Frank did all the drawings, and helped mum with the running of the job. I have no knowledge of the financial arrangements, but I assume dad would have reimbursed the company for the time Frank spent on these endeavours.

> It is clear that Frank and mum got on very well together, and I have no recall of anything dad ever said which would suggest he held Frank in anything but the highest regard. He was of course known to me as Mr. Paice in those days.

> So, what are my memories of Frank himself? I left Scotch College in 1940, and then went to South Australia working with brother Chris on the Morgan-Whyalla

water pipeline. I stayed there till the end of 1942, and then joined the RAAF. Dad died in 1943, there was a bust up between the Board and my brother Ken, which resulted in his resignation. Finally the brothers Hume started their own company in 1946. We did pretty well, and in 1958 Humes bought us out. I remained as manager of our company for three years, then resigned and went onto the Melbourne Stock Exchange.

So, my connection with Frank was as a boy up till 1940, and then nothing [again] until 1958 to 1961. In the last period, Frank was Editor of Hume News, and I recall writing at least two articles for him. Consequently, I did not have a lot to do with him on a day-to-day basis.

I always saw Frank as a good looking, quiet, softly spoken, nice man. I never recall him raising his voice. He had fine manners, and was certainly of great help to my mum.

I was aware of his keen interest in local government, and that he became Mayor of Nunawading. The [Nunawading Reporter] articles you have sent confirm that he and Olga really enjoyed their 'top dog' status — and I would think Frank would have done a very good job as Mayor.

I am sorry if I have not been able to give you better details of "This is your life Frank Paice" but when I came to think it out, my personal experiences with him were not large. Sadly, my four brothers are all dead, and without doubt they could have given you a better picture than I have been able to do. Such is life.

Best wishes, David

23 Florrie's condition revealed

London — September 26, 2003

My research into the court revelations about Florrie's vaginal obstruction has recently taken me onto websites for women with Androgen Insensitivity Syndrome (AIS). The more I learn of this condition, the more likely it seems that AIS — or something very similar — was Florrie's problem. As she apparently had no vagina, she might have been CAIS, a person with the complete form of AIS. This would confirm that the earlier guesses at Florrie's medical problem were wrong.

As luck would have it, BBC Television has just repeated *A Boy Who Became a Girl* – a documentary by the BBC's *Horizon* team about people with intersex conditions. It is a fascinating programme, and my attention is particularly caught by what is said by one of the contributors, an eminent urologist and specialist on intersex children, Mr Philip G. Ransley.

I track him down to his consulting rooms in London and he generously agrees to see me after he has finished the day's medical appointments.

Mr Ransley flicks through my files and studies photographs of Florrie and is quick to declare that she is "a classic CAIS victim".

Through my earlier research into AIS I have already discovered that all foetuses begin life as female, but those with XY chromosomes are destined to become male as the pregnancy progresses. Those with XX chromosomes continue to develop as females. Mr Ransley explains the process when a foetus is XY:

> The body only becomes male if everything works correctly downstream. What the Y chromosome does is direct the gonad to become a testis [testicle], and if you don't have a Y chromosome, the gonad becomes an ovary. The testis produces first of all a substance that makes all the female bits go away – the fallopian tubes,

the uterus and the vagina. All go away under the influence of a hormone called a mullerian inhibiting substance, which is produced by the testes. The testes also produce testosterone which makes you male, which makes the phallus grow, and turns you into a man.

At puberty, when the testes also pour out testosterone again, you grow a beard and get hair under your arms, your voice breaks, your phallus grows and so on. Testosterone is the key hormone that makes you a man, but for testosterone to work, it must circulate in the blood and latch onto a "receptor". It has to get onto that receptor to get inside the cell to make all the metabolic activities happen.

Mr Ransley then explains Complete Androgen Insensitivity Syndrome in more detail:

CAIS is brought about by the fact that although the foetus has masses of testosterone circulating in the blood it has no receptors. A receptor is a protein on the surface of the cell. Now, for your penis to grow, the testosterone must get into your penis, get to the cell in the penis, latch onto the receptor and get inside the cell.

Once it's inside the cell, the testosterone dictates the DNA in that cell to become active and for that cell to grow and multiply and so on. That's how the penis gets bigger. If the testosterone activity is blocked and can't get inside the cell, it just washes past and never has any influence. So in CAIS, the body, although it has made testes, which it was directed to do by the Y chromosome, and those testes produce testosterone which circulates in the body, it has no effect, while the other hormone from the testes has meanwhile got rid of all the female bits inside. It's got rid of the fallopian tubes, the uterus and 90% of the vagina.

With CAIS, your body appears on the outside as a woman because it has had no influence to make it look like a man. So when you look at the external genitalia, they look like a completely normal female: a tiny clitoris, the urethroid [outlet for urine] at the base of the clitoris and a vaginal opening. But the vagina doesn't go anywhere because the other hormone from the testes has got rid of 90% of it. It's only one or two cms long. So this fits exactly with what Frank Paice was describing [in his divorce deposition].

I put it to Mr Ransley that Florrie might not have been CAIS; perhaps it was simply that her vagina was blocked. He is quick to point out that if it were just that, there would have been nowhere for the blood to go when she began menstruating. She would have blown up inside and there would have been a crisis at puberty requiring surgery. There is no indication that Florrie required such surgery.

Mr Ransley also mentions that women with CAIS don't normally have pubic hair. This again raises questions about why Florrie's parents seemed not to have realised that something was unusual about Florrie. Mr Ransley isn't at all surprised by this question:

They probably didn't know. They probably had no idea because externally she would have appeared completely normal as a female. She would have developed breasts – not big ones – but she would have been very tall because she would have been male height. Because she looked so normal on the outside, apart from the lack of pubic hair, probably no-one knew there was a problem.

I raise the matter of Florrie not having menstruated. Surely her mother, at least, would have noticed that? Mr Ransley points out that it is not that unusual for a woman not to menstruate. There could be lots of different reasons for the lack of periods, one of these being that Florrie was so thin. He also isn't surprised that a lack of pubic or underarm hair had not raised worrying questions in Florrie's family:

How many people would have known that? It was maybe limited. Probably even her mother had never seen her daughter's genitalia since she was probably 12 years old. She would have been taught that this is concealed and you don't expose it. Even today, I see children here about 12 or 14 and I will very often ask the mother if she wants to have a look at whatever we are looking at. She will say "yes I would. I haven't seen it for a long time". Kids, even today, are taught in many families, particularly the religious families, to keep their genitalia concealed.

Mr Ransley's thoughts on this are confirmed as he studies the 1914 studio photograph of Florrie with the rest of her family. All the women are demurely wearing high-necked, long-sleeved dresses that reach down to the ankle:

Looking at that family, I would suspect that the mother had never seen her daughter naked from the age of 12. During her childhood they would have thought her genitalia to be completely normal. To be honest, you need look no further for diagnosis. It is screaming out that she is CAIS.

Mr Ransley expresses some sympathy for Florrie's mother:

To be honest, I suspect her mother was innocent, in a way. She could not have been aware of the implications of her daughter's development. At the time there was a tremendous amount of ignorance.

I think that the problem of intersex has been with us in all human history. Of that there can be no doubt. And of particular difficulty are the males who are very poorly developed and who have terrible things wrong with their penises.

My aunt, when one of these very unfortunate babies was born, would say "Oh dear... Another one for the [Catholic] church". I think that the church probably provided an amazing social service for – homosexuals obviously – but also for the sexually inadequate where they didn't have to compete [sexually]. So, okay, here's a daughter who's not quite right, but she's not bad... She may not be able to have babies but being devoted to the church they won't be too interested in sex.

Mr Ransley studies Florrie's psychiatric reports from the Mont Park asylum and the post mortem after her death in 1950 — some years before AIS had been fully identified and recognised as a medical condition:

> What a pity… I mean the post mortem report… The post mortem pathologist's brief would have been to establish the cause of death [lobar pneumonia]. He wouldn't have looked any further and wouldn't have known what he was looking at anyway, unless he came across testicles. They would have been inside the abdomen.

Though Florrie gave the appearance of being a woman, I wondered whether she felt like one. Mr Ransley was unsure because he didn't usually treat CAIS patients once they reached adulthood. He did, however, explain about the significance of testosterone during preg-nancy:

> It is hugely important. Your body and my body were exposed to testosterone in the womb then immediately after we were born, for about three months, the blood surges with testosterone. If you measured the testosterone at two or three months in a male baby, it would be the same level as in a randy 15 year old. You can't do much with it at that age [as a baby] but what it does is alter the brain. It is during that period that the brain gets altered to a male orientation.

But as Mr Ransley had already pointed out, the testosterone would have had no impact on Florrie. On the whole, his experience was that CAIS women were "a little bit masculine, but not very much". He felt that it was important that I get in touch with the AIS Support Group in Britain. I agree to do this.

London — November 4, 2003

I write to the AIS Support Group, explaining my background and the purpose of my *God's Triangle* projects, but I get no reply. It is not a real surprise as the group's media guidelines indicate some bad experiences with the media:

> We have had some dealings with newspapers, magazines and TV film companies in recent years, with mixed results. It has led to some helpful coverage which has normalized the conditions by removing some of the stigma that has surrounded them. However, our cooperation has also been abused by inaccurate medical de-tails, sensationalized stories, and inappropriate or offensive headlines or voice-overs added without consultation etc.

I decide to let it rest for the time being.

24 The jigsaw takes shape

Having gained access to Florrie Cox's divorce file and identified with some certainty her medical condition, the *God's Triangle* project was put on the back burner to allow me to deal with other commitments. After this pause, the research resumes and more gaps in the jigsaw are filled.

London — July 2005

Ros Gooden, now in retirement in Adelaide, is holidaying in the United Kingdom. She stays with us for four days, and this allows us to review our findings over the previous years.

One interesting discussion concerns Florrie's motivation. Did she go to Bengal primarily to marry Frank? Or was her main concern the spreading of God's word? Ros is convinced that it was the former. If Florrie's prime interest had been missionary work, she could have gone as a single woman. This would have given her greater status on the missionary field, rather than being regarded as "just a missionary wife". That is not to imply that Florrie's only objective was marriage. It is obvious that she genuinely wished to help the people of Bengal and play a part in the spread of Christianity.

Though it has no significant bearing on my investigations, Ros explains some of the practicalities involved in becoming a missionary. Ros herself didn't go to Bengal as a missionary until the mid-1960s, but even then she took with her a total of 11 sealed 44-gallon oil drums packed with supplies, including enough toilet paper to last four or five years until she was due for her first furlough. Needless to say, she travelled to Bengal by ship, rather than air.

London — February 14, 2006

A visitor to our house spots that the mouse for one of our computers is set up for left-hand use. "Left handed, I see," then he jokingly adds: "The mark of the Devil".

I ask him where he got that from and he tells me it came from a friend in Northern Ireland who had been brought up in a convent. He says she was badly beaten by the nuns every time she used her left hand. That was just 20 years ago.

This story provides further evidence that Olga Johnston's religious hostility to left-handed people was not so unusual.

London — March 13, 2006

I email David Hume to seek his comments about the revelation that Olga slept with a revolver under her pillow. He replies immediately:

> Olga always seemed to be a LARGE lady to me, and quite overpowering — so, it is not unexpected that she did not rate high in my popularity stakes. I can well imagine her sleeping with a revolver under the pillow.

> I never saw her in my 'mature' years, but can imagine she would have revelled in being Lady Mayoress [of Nunawading] — but probably not as much as she would have preferred the reversed role where Frank would have been number two. But, of course, I have no grounds to make this remark.

Melbourne — May 4, 2006

I have lunch with Professor Garry Warne of the Royal Children's Hospital in Melbourne. He specialises in Androgen Insensitivity Syndrome and liaises with AIS support groups. He willingly agrees to help me with my research. As a start, he contacts a Partial AIS woman in Victoria, asking her if she will talk to me.

Melbourne — May 19, 2006

David Hume has been going through some of his sister Bernie's papers and comes across this fascinating comment:

> I should say that whilst in India [circa 1923] our parents stayed with a Mr and Mrs Paice in a charming bungalow. These people later returned to Australia and lived in Blackburn. Mr P. was a long and valued employee of Hume's, but poor Mrs Paice hated the change from India and bemoaned her fate at every possible occasion. At the age of 17, I was invited to dinner and remember a dreadful argument taking place at the dinner table.

This fits with earlier comments about Olga, but why did she hate being back in Australia? Was it because she was no longer a lady of leisure, surrounded by ever-present and ever-obedient servants? Was it because she had developed a deep and genuine love for India? Was it because she feared her past being exposed? Or was it something else entirely? We can only guess.

London — May 25, 2006

As suggested by Garry Warne, I am in touch with the woman with Partial AIS. Her story is very interesting and relevant to the story of Florrie Cox. To protect her identity, I will call her Valerie in these extracts from my notes:

> Valerie is 75 years old. Born and married in England. Moved to Australia in the 1960s. Well spoken, relaxed, intelligent and frank, with a positive view of life. Daughter of a clergyman who died when she was young.

> Had one sibling — a sister, we'll call Beryl — who remained in England and also had AIS. Beryl became a manic depressive. Married for 11 years, but divorced after her mental problems became too much for her. Died from a kidney complaint after failing to get treatment because of a fear of doctors.

> Valerie said it was impossible to know what, if any, link there was between Beryl's mental condition and being AIS. She said she and her sister had very different characters.

> She believes her mother was an AIS carrier and thinks that as three of her aunties never married, they may also have been AIS, or at least were carriers. She was very curious to know if Florrie's sisters were able to have children, as it was likely that her mother or grandmother was an AIS carrier. I told her there were three sisters, two of whom had children, the third having died from TB aged 22 and unmarried.

Valerie went on to explain that she and her husband had normal sexual relations:

> She said that she has a normal length vagina, but has no internal female organs and, of course, she has never menstruated. She has always been able to have normal sexual intercourse and had normal vaginal lubrication. She and her husband were aware when they married that she could not have children and they adopted three children in Australia. She and her husband now have several grandchildren. She understood that her sister had a good sex life and assumed that she also had normal vaginal lubrication.

> Neither she nor her sister had much pubic hair – an AIS indicator.

> She had always felt and thought like a woman. As children, she and her sister always opted for "girlie" things.

Valerie and Beryl only discovered their AIS condition by accident:

> Although Valerie knew she and her sister weren't entirely normal, she did not realise she had AIS until she returned to England 10 years ago to help sort

out her sister. While in a doctor's waiting room she picked up a magazine and read an article about Complete AIS. From this, she recognised the condition that she and her sister had. She told the doctor.

It was then discovered she had two undescended testes in her lower body and these were removed. When I asked why these hadn't been noticed before, she said both she and her sister were born with double hernias and this had caused the confusion. She said the testes had never given her any pain during intercourse — AIS women often complain when pressure is applied to their testes, which usually sit above the pelvic bone – and this was probably because they proved to be "a mish-mash" of ovarian and testicular tissue.

Asked about whether her religious background had made life more difficult for her and her sister, she said she didn't think it had. But she was a bit shocked that when she told her mother about them having AIS, she had replied "I'm glad your father never knew". She said her own condition had made her tolerant of homosexuals, knowing that despite some interpretations of the bible, they had no control over their sexual orientation.

She said AIS women would know that there was something wrong with them, but often never knew what it was and would feel very alone in the world.

She said that women with Partial AIS often have more difficult lives, because they have partly made the transition from female to male in the womb and when born appeared to be of mixed gender. In some cases, doctors "assigned" a gender to them, based on what appeared to be the most likely one. As a result, some Partial AIS children would be brought up as boys when they thought of themselves as girls and this caused enormous emotional confusion and anger.

Later in the day an email arrives from Professor Warne, telling me that he has recommended that the AIS Support Group in the UK make contact with me. Soon after an email arrives from the AISSG, offering to post a message on its Yahoo Group news exchange seeking information for my project. I accept this invitation with enthusiasm.

London — May 30, 2006

I am thrilled to receive an email from the United States telling me that my message has been passed on to the American and Canadian AIS Support Group.

London — June 2, 2006

I write to my family and tell them of the progress I have been making with my research into AIS and my attempts to "get into the head" of Great Aunt Florrie. I report that I have had some fascinating and helpful responses to my AIS Support Group message, not just from Britain but also from Australia and North America:

Because of the sensitivity of the subject, I suggested that respondents might prefer to talk to Rosemary, but they have been quite happy to talk frankly to me about their condition and the traumas they faced. Surprisingly, I learnt that despite more relaxed sexual attitudes that have existed in recent decades some of the women went through most of their lives not being told the truth about their condition.

Several women complained that they had been raised in very religious families and they resented the restrictions put on honest discussion of their condition. Another thing that has emerged is that Great Aunt Florrie was probably in a minority of CAIS sufferers in that she was born without a vagina. Several women who have been in touch reported that they were happily married, had normal and enjoyable sex lives, and had successfully adopted children.

I am now hoping to hear from someone whose condition replicates that of Great Aunt Florrie, because what happened to her must have left her very isolated and utterly desolate.

London — June 5, 2006

I report back to Garry Warne about the responses I have had and ask him what percentage of CAIS women are born with no vagina at all. The answer, he says, is "about five percent". So that means Florrie was in a small minority within a minority. In other words, her situation was extremely rare.

London — July 21, 2006

I receive a very touching and rather tentative phone call from a CAIS woman here in Britain. She spoke initially to Rosemary and sought re-assurance that it was okay for her to talk to me. Rosemary told her that it was fine, but even so, the conversation was sometimes rather circumspect. I shall call her Mary to protect her identity. I made these notes:

Mary is a shy, softly-spoken woman in her 40s. She converted to Christianity at the age of 15. As a Christian, she had great sympathy for my great aunt's situation and felt she might be able to help me 'get into her head'. She admitted it had taken her some time to summon up the courage to phone me.

Mary was married at the age of 18 and was a virgin when married because of her Christian beliefs. Her husband is also a Christian. She regarded the marriage [of 25 years] as a success.

She knew there was something wrong with her when she was 10. She was told that her aunt also had the problem. But she didn't know this was CAIS until many years later.

When she was 17, she went to see a woman gynaecologist. She was told she had no womb, but wasn't told that she didn't have a proper vagina. The gynaecologist was mystified why her blood tests showed unusually high levels of testosterone, and why she did not have any underarm or pubic hair. The doctor had no experience or knowledge of CAIS.

When Mary married, her husband was aware that they couldn't have children, but they were not aware she did not have a proper vagina and therefore couldn't consummate the marriage in the traditional way. She and her husband decided they wouldn't adopt children, and my impression was that they took this view because they felt that if God had wanted them to have children, she would not have her condition.

At one point, she returned to the gynaecologist who gave her some dilators without explaining properly how these might help (her shyness probably played a part in this). It was only after she was put in touch with the AIS Support Group that she had the confidence and knowledge to use the dilators to good effect to enlarge her vagina. This worked sufficiently well for her marriage to be consummated in the traditional way three years ago.

Mary made it clear in her own circumspect way that she and her husband had used mutual masturbation as a satisfactory substitute for traditional sex. I told her that I had decided against implying that Frank and Florrie had indulged in oral sex. Her view was that this was unlikely around that period of the 1900s, but in any case, she said oral sex would have been a progression only if they had first become comfortable with mutual masturbation.

Mary admitted that she had wondered why God had "done this to me" and whether it was some sort of punishment. It had also challenged her relationship with God. Mary said that she had not been able to find anything in the bible that suggested God would disapprove of sexual relations that departed from the traditional 'missionary position'.

London — August 2, 2006

An email arrives from a CAIS woman in Ireland. She tells me that she and her twin sister are both CAIS and that she has two non-CAIS sisters, though they might be carriers.

She and her sister were diagnosed with the condition when they were 16 or 17. She knew something was wrong because neither she nor her sister had periods or pubic hair. She had once tried to insert a Tampax and discovered that her vagina was just three inches deep.

The discovery of her condition had resulted in "very, very hard times", but she had been given much support by her family.

25 The AIS story first hand

London — September 11, 2006

The United Kingdom AIS Support Group asks me to be a guest speaker at next year's annual conference of the group. Both Rosemary and I are invited, but I am warned that the invitation is subject to none of the members objecting to our presence at what is normally a private gathering. I advise that we would both be happy to attend if this meets with the approval of those attending.

London — April 13, 2007

The *God's Triangle* project has been on the back burner again for several months, but today the AIS Support Group contacts me to   confirm the invitation to their conference — to be held in June.

London — June 30, 2007

Rosemary and I attend the AIS Support Group annual conference. We are made most welcome.

There were about 40 women attending. Of these, 17 were Complete AIS, ranging in age from 13 to 64. The rest were mostly Partial AIS or mothers of AIS women.

Had we not known the purpose of the conference, it would have been reasonable to assume that we were joining any non-specific gathering of women. The only difference that might be noticed was they were a little above average height because of their male XY chromosomes.

My speech, which summarised what I have learnt so far, attracted lots of sensible questions about how I intended to tell the story of *God's Triangle*.

A vote was taken on whether Rosemary and I would be permitted to attend the private afternoon session and we were flattered that not one person opposed this.

The afternoon session was both very sad and fascinating as the women sat in a circle and exchanged experiences and advice that was frank, sensible and encouraging. The predominating message that came across to us was that the women hated being thought of as freaks and just wanted to lead as normal a life as possible. Some of the AIS women still felt they couldn't tell anyone outside the support group about their condition.

We felt enormous sympathy for these women, but as I pointed out, at least they had their support group and some medical understanding of their condition. Poor Florrie Cox had nothing. When she was alive, her condition hadn't even been identified and the reaction among family and friends to her plight was primarily one of embarrassment.

London — July 30, 2010

Initially, it was my intention to use pseudonyms for all the main individuals in *God's Triangle*, but as the project progresses, it becomes clearer to me that this would undermine the authority and impact of the story. It might also result in a counter-productive guessing game.

I consult Ros Gooden and she agrees that no harm can be done to any living person by using the correct names. At the same time, Rosemary presses me to write this book, so that there is a detailed and chronological record of the story and how it was uncovered.

London — September 3, 2010

I phone a cousin in Melbourne, Alan Cox, a son of one of Florrie's brothers, Charles Cox. He has recollections of both Florrie and her mother, Amelia.

Alan's memories of Amelia, who was his aunt, are vague. He says that in her later years his family would occasionally visit her at her home. She would be in a rocking chair with the blinds pulled down. It was very dark in the house and he remembers that it would take some time for his eyes to adjust.

Alan didn't know Florrie until her later years, so is unable to enlighten me much about what she was like in the 20 years or so between being divorced and when her mental problems began to get on top of her.

He tells me that in the period preceding Florrie's admission to the Mont Park asylum she would alternate between the homes of his father and his uncle, my grandfather Arthur J. G. Cox. He recalls that she spent a month or two at a time in each house. After Florrie was admitted to Mont Park, the family would visit her but she sometimes barely recognised them. Alan says she was "not with it" for much of the time.

Alan doesn't think he ever went inside the asylum buildings, as the family usually saw Florrie in the gardens. Alan says he was also a member of a cricket team that sometimes played in the grounds of Mont Park and this could be disturbing, with inmates "looking mad" and appearing out of storm drains and other places. He also remembers some inmates being behind bars or in cages.

In the course of my discussion with Alan, I am reminded of a conversation I had a few years ago with my mother's twin sister, Eelin. She knew Florrie reasonably well before she became mentally ill and described her as "a lovely lady". What a pity I left it too late to contact others who would have known Florrie when she was in her thirties and forties.

26 The journey ends

And so we come to the conclusion of my journey of discovery, though disappointingly not to the completion of the *God's Triangle* jigsaw. I have to accept there are gaps in Great Aunt Florrie's story — gaps that may remain unfilled.

My greatest disappointment is missing the opportunity to talk to former missionary Cyril Baldwin before he died. Cyril, as explained in Chapter 18, died taking his personal knowledge of the scandal to his grave. Unless someone comes up with some long-hidden or long-overlooked documents that reveal all, a certain amount of what happened to Florrie, Frank Paice and Olga Johnston in India will remain educated conjecture.

Given that the Baptist Church no longer appears to have detailed documents about the affair, the most likely sources would have been Hedley and Elsie Sutton, Frank Paice or one of the siblings of Olga Johnston.

Hedley and wife Elsie seemed determined not to leave any trace in their extensive files. Frank Paice could well have kept some relevant records, but son Paul found the huge volume of files stored in a garden shed overwhelming and threw most of them out.

As for Olga's brothers and sisters, they are long dead and any knowledge of the story of *God's Triangle* probably died with them. The same applies to the missionaries working for, or alongside, the Baptists in Bengal at that time.

Putting aside the disappointing unknowns, much has been learned.

I am confident that Florrie married Frank in good faith, not knowing that she couldn't have sexual intercourse or bear children. Frank would also have been unaware of his wife-to-be's condition.

It is an open question whether Florrie's mother, Amelia Cox, suspected that something was not quite right. She must have known that her daughter was not menstruating, but such were the sexual ignorance and social restraints back then, she may not have understood its full significance. Anyway, even if she did have a clear idea of the link between menstruation and reproduction, Amelia would mostly likely not have wanted to inform her daughter of the brutal fact that she would probably be childless.

Engaged but separated

As already explained, Frank and Florrie spent their engagement apart, so would have had none of the intimate moments that would normally have taken place between two people who had declared an intention to marry.

Put another way, they would not have had the opportunity to explore each other's bodies, even if this "petting" would have fallen short of actual sexual intercourse. In any case, evidence points to neither of them wishing to cross any sexual barriers until the marriage knot was tied.

There is no doubt that Florrie was born with a very rare form of Complete Androgen Insensitivity Syndrome (CAIS) – a condition not given its name until after her death.

It would have been incredibly lonely for Florrie in India and after her return to Australia. Though she did her best to carry on a relatively normal life back in Melbourne, she cannot have failed to be distressed by the fact that her circumstances were an embarrassing secret, while Frank prospered and rose to prominence in business and public life, first in India and then back in Melbourne.

It must also have been deeply hurtful for Florrie to learn through a birth announcement in the *Melbourne Argus* that Frank had finally achieved his ambition to become a father when Paul was born in Melbourne in 1927.

Given the medical ignorance that prevailed at the time, Florrie could easily have believed, or at least feared, that she was the only woman in the world born without a vagina. Being deeply religious, Florrie may well have imagined that her God was punishing her for some unspecific deed. Added to that, her mother, and possibly her father, were embarrassed by what happened and couldn't, or wouldn't, show parental sympathy and support. No wonder she finally succumbed to mental illness.

Sadly, I began my research into the story of *God's Triangle* far too late to talk to Florrie's friends and associates. This would have given me some insight into how she handled her situation during the 20 years or so between the divorce and when her depression became intolerable.

As for Frank and Olga, they were most likely friends — perhaps more than just friends — from the early days of their time in Bengal. They would have been studying Bengali alongside each other in Calcutta for much of their first two years as missionaries. However, there is no conclusive evidence when this friendship developed into a more intense sexual relationship.

My best guess is that they became lovers around the time Frank, Florrie and Olga went on holiday together in Kashmir in 1916 and around the time Frank told the Supreme Court that he stopped attempting to have intercourse with Florrie.

A blind eye to the affair?

In such a tiny, socially-incestuous community, the unhappy circumstances must have been noted at a reasonably early stage by Hedley Sutton and his fellow missionaries. At the very least, the servants would have known that Frank and Florrie were no longer sharing a bedroom.

Perhaps everyone was in denial. Perhaps they just looked the other way in what they felt were the best interests of the church, its missionaries and, above all, the missionary finances. Missionary funding had long been a struggle. As far back as August 1915, *Our Indian Field* was reporting cutbacks in missionary activities as a result of "the uphill financial fight on account of the war".

High on my list of possibilities, initially, was that Olga found herself pregnant on her return to Melbourne on furlough in October 1917. But the more I examine the timescale, the more difficulty I see this having happened – not least because Olga's funding-raising efforts in Australia were still being applauded five months after beginning her furlough.

That would hardly have happened if she were pregnant. As a consequence, another possibility moves to the top of my list: that a love letter written by Frank or Olga fell into the wrong hands in Melbourne or Bengal. This might well have made an illicit relationship impossible for the church authorities to ignore.

There is also a scenario that I had not considered until now: might Florrie have tried to commit suicide on finding a love letter from Olga, or been confronted with other news of the affair?

This would certainly qualify as "an unhappy event", as mentioned in the church Minutes (Chapter 11). It might also explain why the mission board expressed a hope that the marriage could be repaired.

The hasty court case

It remains a mystery how it was possible for the Supreme Court to bend the rules, allowing what amounted to a "quickie" divorce in an age when such proceedings normally took years.

A further question is why it was felt necessary to rush the case through? Frank, it is known, wanted to take up a job in Calcutta. This wasn't stated when the proceedings were initiated just a couple of months after arriving in disgrace in Melbourne with Florrie. Less than a month later, while the divorce was still being considered by the court, Frank was on his way back to India, possibly with Olga.

One explanation for the speedy hearing could be that Mr Justice Hood accepted Frank's declaration that he and Florrie had "lived entirely apart" for the last two years they spent in Faridpur. This could have been seen by the court as the official separation period.

Calcutta would not have seemed an ideal future home for Frank and Olga because of the possibility they would bump into former mission-ary colleagues. However, the chances of this would have been lessened because they would then have been moving in business rather than religious circles in a city with a huge population. Additionally, Frank switched to the Presbyterian Church, while Olga rejected organised Christianity totally.

Florrie's options

It could be argued that Florrie would have been able to divorce Frank for adultery, assuming this could have been proved. But Florrie clearly knew that the prime reason for the failure of the marriage was her physical disability, even though she was unable to fully understand what it was. She was a kindly soul who retained her Christian faith throughout her life, so it is reasonable to suppose that she didn't wish to cause additional embarrassment for the families or the church.

Who arranged the cover-up and why? The Baptist Church was un-deniably at the heart of it. It would have been terrified that publicity would have sullied its reputation and caused a loss of public funding.

Both were reasonable fears. Society in the early 1900s was deeply conservative and would have been scandalised by what happened. There would have been little understanding for Florrie, Frank or Olga. Judgemental attitudes could easily have strangled the flow of essential donations to the church and its missionary activities — especially at a time when Australia and the rest of the British Empire were on their economic knees because of the crippling cost of the Great War.

The role of the Freemasons

The support of the Freemasons in the cover-up would have been hugely important, if not vital. The Masons, with their penchant for secrecy and their powerful connections in the Protestant churches and business worlds, would have been ideal partners to help the church keep the story under wraps.

As my research revealed, the head of the Baptist Mission Society, the Rev. Joseph Goble, was a high-ranking Freemason, even though the Baptists often frowned on its adherents being involved in their type of organisation. The founder of Hume Pipes & Engineering, Walter Hume, was also a keen and noted Mason and was the person who hired Frank.

Frank would have been a magnificent asset to Hume's new India division. He had done training as an engineer, he had a notable management track record with the Faridpur Industrial School and he was not just familiar with the ways of India but was a fluent Bengali-speaker. In short, he was perfect for a high-level management position in a new and thrusting company.

I accept that the presiding judge, Mr Justice Hood, was not a Freemason and I further accept that he rejected an application to have the hearings take place behind closed doors. In that case why weren't the divorce details plastered in voyeuristic detail across the pages of the scandal-obsessed Melbourne *Truth*? And why did it not even get a mention in the detailed court listings in the Melbourne *Argus*? Or even discreet coverage in the Melbourne *Age*? Or a mention in the after-noon paper, the Melbourne *Herald*?

The silence of the press

My conclusion is that the publishers and editors of the newspapers simply chose not to cover the story, either out of sympathy for the

Baptist Church or under pressure from the Freemasons, or both.

Mr Justice Hood then nailed the lid on the coffin of secrecy, so to speak, by ruling that no-one should ever be permitted to see the contents of the divorce file. What was so compelling that he should have felt that to be necessary and that his order would be reinforced by another judge in 2000?

The irony is that had I not encountered these curious obstructions, Florrie's story might have been relegated to little more than a few vaguely-interesting paragraphs in my family history.

My suspicions about the ban are supported by the recent discovery by Rosemary that one of her relatives, Henry Thomas Hellings, sought a divorce in Melbourne in 1919. This hearing took place less than three months after Frank and Florrie's annulment was granted. It was also in the Supreme Court of Victoria. It was also presided over by Mr Justice Hood. So why was my great aunt's "juicy" case ignored by the press, while the *Melbourne Argus* devoted several paragraphs to the Hellings divorce that involved a wife's bigamy?

The answer probably is that the Hellings case did not have wider issues beyond the three parties involved, while the Paice hearings, had they become public knowledge, would have caused ructions and had financial consequences for the Baptist Church and its missionaries.

The story I have recounted and some of the views I have expressed could attract criticism. The sensitive nature of this story makes that inevitable. The truth sometimes embarrasses. I fully recognise that, but I also contend that to skirt around the facts would make this book an exercise with no historical or social value.

Did the cover-up matter?

It has been argued that Florrie's tragic story is of little interest or importance outside the extended family or the Baptist Church. I don't agree. If you haven't found *God's Triangle* interesting, then I offer my apologies. But I retain my certainty that the story is important, with many lessons about religious and social tolerance to be learned and acted upon. It may sound pompous, but I believe it is a story with some universal messages.

The lessons are not just about Florrie. They concern a wider group of people – not only women with AIS – who through no fault of their own have difficult lives, or who won't or can't conform in some way.

There are also lessons about racial attitudes and openness in society.

The modern world is not perfect, but those who urge a return to "the good old days" are deluding themselves, as I hope this story has abundantly demonstrated.

I have used "scandal" as a description of what happened. But was it a scandal if the general public never got to hear about it? Well, yes it was. It rocked the Baptist missions and the families concerned to such an extent that Frank Paice's brother, George, and his family felt the need to flee to a remote part of South Australia. The families of George and Frank were never reconciled, and George's entire family went to their graves refusing to discuss the story behind the rift.

As for the cover-up, was it all that important when compared with the cover-up of sexual abuse that still plagues the Roman Catholic Church and some other religious institutions? Again, my answer is "yes". It was, of course, very different from the devastating and profoundly-evil sexual abuse cover-ups, but it was a cover-up nevertheless and a very successful one in a society that proudly proclaimed itself to have a transparent and honest judicial system.

Though the intentions of those who organised the *God's Triangle* cover-up may well have been honourable, I am satisfied they were misguided. No doubt there were some who persuaded themselves that the primary purpose was to protect Florrie as an individual, but my cumulative impression is that her welfare came a poor second to the desire to protect the combined reputations of the Baptist Church, its missionary service and the families involved in the affair.

It should be stressed that while my focus has been on the behaviour of the Baptist Church, I am convinced that if other churches had been faced with a similar crisis, they would have exhibited the same defensive determination to see that it didn't get into the public arena.

The victims

Who were the primary victims in *God's Triangle?* Florrie, of course. And Frank? Yes. But Olga? Well, she is more of a grey area, so to speak. Olga's writings in the missionary magazines strongly indicate that she went to Bengal full of religious fervour, but by the time she married Frank she had lost her faith and never regained it. This must have placed a continuing strain on their marriage in view of the fact that Frank continued to be a believer, although with a different Protestant church.

I cannot establish beyond reasonable doubt that Olga was the driving force behind her affair with Frank, but that is my supposition. It seems likely that Florrie was referring to Olga when she made the claim to a psychiatrist at Mont Park asylum that within two days of her marriage, another woman pushed her aside and said she would see that she was divorced so that the husband could marry her instead.

This recollection may have been no more than fantasy or confusion brought on by Florrie's mental state, or she simply invented it to hide what really happened. It is undeniable, though, that Olga had a well-deserved reputation as a forceful woman who liked to get her own way.

There could, therefore, be at least an essence of truth in what Florrie told the psychiatrist. In some respects it doesn't matter because the circumstances were such that if Olga didn't complete the triangle with Frank and Florrie, it might well have been some other woman.

Frank, who was widely considered to be "a good man", must have faced great torment and temptations, having no sexual outlet in his marriage and knowing that Florrie could not bear him his much-desired children. Frank's reported statement to son Paul (Chapter 1) that he and Florrie had been divorced because "she did not tell me she could not have babies" would indicate that Frank felt a sense of betrayal. This feeling, I believe, was misguided, but given the circumstances at the time, it would be understandable.

One thing is certain: Olga was a complex, often difficult, character. She got her man in the end, but there is powerful evidence that her marriage to Frank was not particularly successful or happy. Arguably, Florrie, Frank and Olga were all victims in their own individual ways.